THE 72 SIGILS

Magic, Insight, Wisdom and Change

Zanna Blaise

THE GALLERY OF
MAGICK

CONTENTS

The Secret of The Names

There are no secrets here. Everything you want to know about the 72 Names of God can be found on the internet. If you're really keen, some books explore the 72 Names in more detail and show you how to meditate on them to clear mental blocks and perform personal miracles. With so much information freely available on this subject, there is no need for this book. Except that there is.

The 72 Names of God are mighty three-letter words, written in Hebrew. When you look at these glorious, mystical words in a specific state of mind, magic happens. The magic happens within you and it is reflected in your world. Scanning your eyes over the Names of God can change your world. Sounds pretty awesome.

There is one small problem – there's lots of misinformation out there. Although there are some first-rate books, and even a few useful websites, there's a lot of poorly researched material that will lead you away from the magic.

This book presents the 72 Names as visual Sigils with associated Words of Power, and detailed instructions for working on inner change and outer magic. The Names of God are offered as a workable system of mystical power.

There are so many books already published on The Names of God, but I hope that this book will bring the light of clarity. I will put the magic of these God Names in your hands. You can base your personal explorations on my research, my knowledge, the expertise of great scholars, the experience of magical workers, and the learning of many that have gone before me, but it is *your experience* of these Sigils of Power that will bring you success, within and without.

Kabbalistic magic is meant to be experienced. No amount of history, dogma or preaching can ever be as powerful as your experience. I urge you to take heed of my explanations, but then experience the Sigils for yourself. Make the magic your own.

Before writing this book I looked at information on the web, as well as a couple of cheap, popular books, along with one rare (very expensive) book and a classic text written by an academic, to see what people currently think about the Names of God. I've been working with these Names for a long time, but I wanted to see what people were saying. In all the books, the Hebrew letters were small and difficult to see. Even the expensive coffee-table book contained letters that were almost impossible to read clearly, displayed in an ugly, modern font. The magic is based on seeing the letter shapes, so you cannot get good results with small, pixelated images or badly drawn letters.

In one book, for example, the letters look something like this:

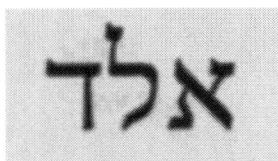

אלד

When you're dealing with a Name of God, it should be written clearly, in a beautiful script, like this:

אלד

I was lead to present each sacred Name as a Sigil. The Name is written as clearly and beautifully as possible, bound by a solid circle to enhance your focus. Each letter was handcrafted, based on traditional techniques and the visual requirements of modern readers. The Names you are looking at are definitely correct and the most accessible that you're ever likely to come across.

If you want to work with the Names of God, you need to *see* the Names of God, so I have made that part of the process as easy as possible. (Some websites even list the wrong Names entirely and are riddled with errors, which is unfortunate, because casual users may then draw the conclusion that these Names have no power. Use the Names as shown in this book and you will *feel* their power.)

The problem with most of the available copies of the Names isn't limited to the look of the letters: each book or website you choose will offer a completely different magical use for each Name. Consider, for instance, the Name Mahash, which looks like this:

מהשי

Mahash is often believed to be a Name of healing. If you read one of the more expensive books, however, it will tell you that the Name will help you to see how *you* are responsible for *your* illness. (That's a form of victim-blaming!) Meanwhile, the academic book explains that the word Mahash can be used to bring rain and that it was used by Moses as a form of attack. How are you supposed to know the correct use of this sacred Name?

The answer comes from the angels. It's possible to find out more about a particular Name by studying the angels that are associated with a Name. Let's take the Name Kahet, which is written like this:

כהת

According to some online sources, Kahet is used to remove negative energy from yourself. The popular Kabbalastic coffee-table book says something similar but also talks about Kahet relieving stress. Another popular website insists this Name will get rid of sadness. The more academic book discusses the use of this Name to get pregnant or even to stop your stomach bursting. These are all interesting possibilities (although I rarely worry about my stomach bursting), but what is the truth? What can this Name actually do for you? To find out, we asked the angels.

I diligently researched the identity of the angelic princes ruling over the Names, as well as other angelic powers associated with the Names, with my trusted magical workers. We communicated with these angels over many years until we have been able to discern the deeper secrets regarding the magical use of the Names. It was revealed to me that the main powers to be found from this Name, Kahet, include the power to see good within a bad situation, and to remove the negative influences of other people. When you need to see beyond the obvious darkness, this Name can help. When somebody is bringing you down, this Name can help you find yourself. Although these powers are real and easy to access, the true secret of the Name is not widely known. This is the case with all 72 Names.

Working with other members of The Gallery of Magick I have studied the Names in depth, communed with the angels and I have experienced the life-changing power of the Names myself. I hope that this system is more useful and meaningful to you than any of the traditional or modern meanings that are often ascribed to the Names. With the help of other experienced magical workers, I have tried to make the magic as simple as possible, beginning with the easiest scanning method we could develop so that you can benefit from the Names of God without ever uttering a word out loud. This method is based on traditional Kabbalistic magic, along with the practical ideas found in more modern methods.

The 72 Sigils of Power can guide you to make the most intuitive and suitable use of each Name, through a mix of wisdom and experience. I created this book because I wanted to publish a text that was based on thorough research and the real experiences of the people I know; people who have benefited from the Names of God every day for many years. Every sacred Name in this book has been explored and tested for decades by me, and by my wise, generous friends. You can be your own authority. Test out these Names of Divine Power and see how they change your life. Fire up the engine of creation.

Working with The Names

Why does this work? If you want to know how the 72 Names were discerned, it's covered briefly in the Appendix. Are these the 'real' Names of God, or is that a traditional label for Words of Power that we use to connect to the Divine? There's a lot of theory if you want to read it, but this book will focus on the practical use of these Names. The Appendix will give you some more detail if it helps you get into the magic.

What's important is that Kabbalists discovered that by scanning your eyes over the letters, these God Names bring about great change. Given that the Names are linked to various angels, it's not really surprising.

The basic method was the inspiration for Damon Brand's popular *Words of Power*, which used both looking at the words and making sounds to bring the Divine Names to life, to access life-changing powers. This book uses a similar approach. However, you can use the Names in this book in two unique and wonderful ways. In Contemplation Magic, you meditate on a Name to bring about inner wisdom, insight, and personal change. In Results Magic, you use the Name to bring about changes in the physical world.

If you want to heal your heart, you would use Contemplation Magic. If you want to calm down an angry person, you would use Results Magic.

It's tempting to think of Contemplation Magic as inner work that changes yourself, and Results Magic as something that changes the outer world. But it's worth remembering that all the inner work you do has an effect on the world around you, and all the Results Magic you do affects your internal process and emotions too.

Contemplation Magic can give you great insight and wisdom, and can help you develop abilities and aspects of your personality. By using Results Magic, the Names can be used to make changes in the world around you. This is the simplest form of magic known, but it works. With each word, you will find an insightful description of its qualities and I will then give you the clues you need to use these words for Contemplation Magic and Results Magic.

You may find it easier to think of Contemplation Magic as being like meditation. It's far easier than meditation and gives you more immediate insight into the depths of your being, but it can be thought of as the meditative side of this process. When you contemplate a Name, you gain insight into yourself, wisdom about who you are, and the ability to bring about change or access the deepest parts of your soul.

You might also want to think of Results Magic as being a little like casting a spell or making a wish. You want something to happen, and you use the Sigil to send your desire into Divine Consciousness. From there, your desire can manifest. It's a way of implanting your desires into the fabric of reality.

Using both Contemplation Magic and Results Magic on the same desire or need will yield the most remarkable results. No surprises there!

You will also find that the distinction between the two types of magic is sometimes extremely subtle. Often, the Results Magic is aimed at creating an internal change. If this is the case, why is there a distinction at all? One reason is that you use different Words of Power to tap into the different aspects of each Name. That's why it's good to have a clear idea of the two different expressions of magic. Another reason is that Results Magic can also be directed at other people. While Contemplation Magic only works on yourself, you can use Results Magic to bring about changes in others. If you're geometrically minded, it might help you to think of Results Magic as a square and Contemplation Magic as a rectangle. They're both rectangles but they're not both squares. So the rules that apply to Results Magic won't also apply to Contemplation Magic, although you can apply the rules of Contemplation Magic to Results Magic.

Let's look at the second Name, Yeli. You will see that under Results Magic there is the power To Recover Joy. This sounds like inner work, but remember you can also guide this magic at others – that's why it's listed as Results Magic. It can make changes to you, but also to other people. With this Name, you can help somebody else to recover joy. It's a bit tricky to grasp at first, but this is a very vital distinction that you need to accept to get the most out of this magic. You are never obliged to use this magic on others. But understanding and accessing the powers offered to you depends on you acknowledging the difference between the possibility of influencing others and only influencing yourself.

The instructions in this book are flexible. I will not tell you exactly how to perform the magic, exactly what to think or feel, or how often to work with the Sigils. I will offer guidance, but as you will see, the magic adapts to you, and you adapt to the magic.

These are Divine Names, being used to connect to your true self and manifest your true will – it cannot be boiled down to a simple formula. It is tempting to write a chapter that tells you that you should perform the magic for five minutes, for eleven days, and then wait for results, but although that could definitely work, there are no set timings for this process, so I'm not going to pretend there are. The magic is much more sensitive to you and your energies. Sometimes the magic is over in minutes. At other times, you will work and develop the magic over many weeks. Only you can know how the magic is working for you.

The process is not complicated, but it is not motionless. You should be prepared to change with the magic, as the magic works to change you in accordance with your deepest needs.

This can be a little unsettling at first. It's far more reassuring to be given a magical system where you carry out set tasks in a set way. That approach is predictable and gives you a feeling of security. One of the reasons that spell-casting is so popular is that it's reassuring to know that if you gather the right herbs, and say a spell at the right phase of the moon, the powers-that-be will be happy that you ticked all their boxes and will bend to your will. This magic is entirely different. There is no one way to get this right. When you work with these Names you will gain a stronger connection to yourself, and the better you know yourself the easier it is for all your desires to manifest. That is the real power of this Divine Magic.

Contemplation or Results?

Soon I'll explain step-by-step what my technique for using the 72 Sigils of God is. But in essence, you scan with your eyes over the shapes of the letters while you think or say a Divine Name. First, I want to triple-check that you understand the difference between what we do for Contemplation Magic and Results Magic.

Contemplation Magic

You choose a Sigil of God that suits your current need.

You scan your eyes over the sigil as instructed.

You say (or think) an extended Divine Word of Power associated with the Name.

While doing this, you focus on a feeling you want to explore, an idea you need to know more about or an aspect of yourself that you want to change.

Magic happens! You gain insights into yourself. Your inner self changes.

Results Magic

You choose a Sigil of God that suits your current need.

You scan your eyes over the sigil as instructed.

You say (or think) a short Divine Word of Power associated with the Name.

While doing this, you focus on a feeling associated with obtaining your desire.

Magic happens! You let go of your result and allow it to manifest.

I've given you this sneak peek, so you know roughly what to expect, but it's absolutely vital that you read the rest of the instructions in full, to get the most out of these sigils. Don't worry, it's absolutely straightforward, but let's not risk confusion.

Over 300 Powers

There are over 300 different powers available in this book because each Name offers several powers and can be used for Contemplation Magic and Results Magic. It's one of the most efficient uses of magical words that I've ever come across and I'm sharing it with you.

You may want to try sitting down and meditating on each word, one after the other, until you've harnessed the powers of all 72 Sigils, and that would be perfectly alright. But if you're reading this book, it's probably because there are certain abilities you want to develop, and changes you want to make, right now. So what if you have actual problems and challenges that you want to deal with?

You may want a better understanding of yourself. You may want to limit or develop an aspect of your personality. Or you may want to create change in your world. You can do all this when you intuit the right Name for your magical purpose and which expression of magic to use - Contemplation or Results or a bit of both.

Sometimes a couple of minutes of meditation with Contemplation Magic is all you need. At other times, you may end up using a whole series of Names and powers to get to the place you want to be. It depends entirely on your personal situation. With a little of my guidance (and I mean a very little), your intuition and the inbuilt feedback from these Names, you'll be a whiz (or is that wizard?) at picking the right Names and Words to manifest your needs and desires.

A quick skim of this book will show you a list of Powers under each Name. Under Contemplation Magic you will see contemplative powers. Under Results Magic, the results-based powers will be listed. Let's run through an example together so that you can feel comfortable going through the rest by yourself: if you look at the first Name, Vehu, you will see that the powers look like this:

Contemplation Magic

VAH-HEH-VAH

Strength and willpower.

Knowledge of what we can manifest.

Unraveling the mystery of how you came to be where you are.

Results Magic

VEH-WHO

To obtain strength when facing a difficult situation.

To manifest a desire.

It only takes a few seconds for you to see that you can use the Name Vehu to improve your inner strength and willpower and to learn about your own ability to manifest. You will also see that you can use this Name to obtain strength in difficult times and to manifest your desires. As you skim through the pages of this book looking at all these listed powers, you will get an intuitive sense about the powers that best suit your immediate needs. It's worth going through the whole book and getting a good idea of all the powers that are on offer to you.

(You might have noticed that the Words of Power VAH-HEH-VAH and VEH-WHO each sit atop a list of powers. For now, ignore them. Yes, words of power like this are important and you'll need them later, but while you're just skimming through the book, looking for the Powers you want to work with, you can leave them be.)

You can start immediately with Results Magic if you like. Let's practice your first ritual together. We'll role-play that you want a new personality trait. A popular request is for more charisma or confidence, so let's look through the book for this:

we find the third Name is Sit, and the Word of Power for Results Magic is SEET, with the power to Take on a New Personality Trait. This is perfect for our purpose, so you can now go ahead and use Results Magic to get yourself more confidence and charisma, and know that it will work. (Feel free to combine this with the tenth Name, Elad, which has the power To Increase Personal Charisma.)

Sometimes, though, it's worth pausing and seeing if there is any Contemplation Magic that might help you get a better grounding. Quite often, it can help your overall plan to gain some insight into your needs. If you understand why you have the need, and why this desired reality is not currently with you, it can open the pathways that are resisting the manifestation of your wants and needs.

Let's progress our role-play so that you might look at the Contemplation powers of the Name Sit, and you will see that it can help you find out more about The Depths of Personality and The Potential For Change. Remember, when working with Contemplation Magic, you aren't just working to discover insights, but also to change aspects of yourself. So you can use the magic to explore what you really need and to make changes to yourself. The wisest course of action here might be to do the following:

1. Use Contemplation Magic to explore the depths of your personality, meditating on your need for more charisma. You may now intuitively understand why you lack confidence and you'll feel the delight of understanding the nature of the charisma you seek.

2. Use Contemplation Magic to increase your inner potential for change. Meditate on your need for transformation, allowing your potential for change to grow. By now you will be ready for the last step.

3. Use Results Magic to give yourself more confidence and charisma, using the powers of Sit and Elad.

Would you do this all at once? You could. You do Step 1 for two minutes, and then follow it straight away with Step 2, finish the whole process with Step 3 and have everything done in ten minutes. However, be open to really spending time (perhaps a week) with Step 1, so that you can enjoy deeper results. Instant change is absolutely fine, but you might enjoy a more substantial bounty for your work if you work a little longer.

In our example of someone seeking a change in personality, it may be beneficial to work on each of the Steps two or three times every day. In the first week, you might perform Step 1 between one and five times a day. Each time you do the working, it might last for a minute or up to fifteen minutes. Step 2 might take a couple of minutes, two times a day, for a week. You might then perform Step 3 for five minutes every day until you feel the change has been etched into your soul.

Are there no firm guidelines? No, there aren't. As I said earlier, I could say to you, perform the magic for two minutes, three times a day for eleven days. Or I could say, perform the magic for ten minutes, for just one day. But it all depends on how you *feel* when performing the magic. This will be explained in greater detail, later, but the reason there are no hard and fast rules is that this magic can change you as you work. You need to feel what the magic is telling you. In this way, it is a far more mystical and involved process than many forms of magic.

It's important to be prepared for change as you work. Still working through our role-play, you might start meditating on your need for charisma, and on day three, during the magic, you gain a great insight - you realize that you don't actually want more charisma, and that your confidence is already high. The only reason you *believed* you had a lack of confidence is because Somebody Else told you so. Don't fail to take advantage of this insight. Act on the message that someone has subjugated you. Accept who you are, and you change your approach to the magic. You now look for the most suitable power in light of your new discovery. You throw out all your old plans and see what you really need to change. Skim through the book again and find the eighth Name, Kahet, and the power To Remove The Negative Influence of Other People.

The magic may work rapidly, or the changes may be slow and subtle. You might perform a whole week of Contemplation Magic and gain no conscious insights into the problem. Do not think of this as failed magic. Conscious awareness is part of this process, but it isn't always essential. If you lay the inner groundwork, *the inner work is done,* and it doesn't matter if you receive no clues. If you get no messages or intuitive leaps, just continue as planned and know that at the level of your soul, something is happening.

Although you may sometimes change your mind about what you want, that isn't always the case. If you did the ritual from our role-play, you might experience everything just the way you'd planned. You might use the first two stages of Contemplation Magic without gaining any obvious conscious clues about who you are, but the inner work is done, so you proceed to the Results Magic and make a change to your personality. Don't expect consistent delivery of the changes you seek. Sometimes it might be instant and other times it might be a gradual transformation or awakening to change.

There is almost a limitless potential for change when you use these Powers with your needs and personality.

Now it's up to you. What power do you want to work with first? Do another skim through the book but this time think about what it is that you want and look at all the different Names and their powers. You may see a power that appeals to you immediately, or you may have to search more methodically to find out what you want to use.

Choosing a Name involves getting an understanding of the Name's overall meaning. I want to make sure that you know what I mean so let's look at the very first Name in this book, Vehu, and see how it might apply.

The overview of this Name is *Manifestation and Strength.* That immediately tells you something about the Name. You should then read the description that elaborates on the power. For Vehu, the description says, '*This Name is concerned with universal unity, and the perception that our strength in the material world can lead to the greatest spiritual growth, while our spiritual growth can lead to great material strength.'* These descriptions are short and sometimes quite obscure. This is deliberate. This is not a recipe book, but an opening to mystical power. Read the descriptions with this in mind, and see if you can gain an intuitive sense of the Name which might help you.

Under Contemplation Magic, for Vehu, you will see that one of the powers listed for this Name is to gain Knowledge of What We Can Manifest. Manifestation is when you bring things into material existence, either by magic or through your ordinary actions. Whether you want to paint a masterpiece, give birth or make more money, you are trying to manifest something in the world. By meditating on this Name, and thinking about the things you want to manifest, you will gain insight into the possibility of manifestation. Is it possible for you to get what you want? This Name will provide you with an insightful answer. Sometimes, the things we want to manifest are not ideal for our progress through this life. At other times, the things we dream of are only just out of reach, and it can be so delightful and reassuring to discover that our goal is not just possible but imminent. When you meditate on this Name you will find out how close the manifestation is to fruition.

I want you to imagine with me that you've spent your whole life dreaming of painting a masterpiece. You want to make a gigantic inspirational leap, and paint something truly unique. You want to make great art. When you meditate on the Name, you may sense that you are a long way from achieving this aim. If so, what do you do? You look for other Names that can help you develop and grow your talent. You can then come back to the Name Vehu and meditate again, to see if your manifestation is getting closer. This isn't fortune telling, but it is a way of seeing how well connected you are to your dreams and desires.

You may also find that when you meditate on a Name, that you gain astonishing insights into your true desires. Let's assume we've done all this work with Vehu and now you may find that you get a sudden realization – the only reason you wanted to paint a masterpiece was to make up for the criticism your drawings received at school, or because you're trying to impress your parents. Letting go of false dreams is far more satisfying than trying to force them to come into being. The great power of Contemplation Magic is that it helps you to know yourself, and develop an inner awareness of what you really want.

But, for now, let's imagine that when you meditate on the Name, you find that the manifestation *is* close to hand, and you gain some insights into what you need to do. You may find that you are ready to bring this artwork into reality. So, let's look again at what Vehu can do: Vehu also has the power to Manifest A Desire. You might want to start working with Results Magic, as you begin work on your masterpiece, using Divine Power to guide your inspiration and creation.

It is not my place to explore every possibility of every power of every Name. If I tried to, I would close you off to many potential powers. You will need to spend some time thinking about the powers and feeling your way around them, to see if they fit. The descriptions and powers may not seem obviously useful to you at first, but when you have a need, or when you want to explore these Names, their powers will be revealed.

I want to run through one more example with you. This time look at the second Name, Yeli, and the power called The Sense of Being Alone. Why would anybody want to contemplate loneliness? There are many good reasons. The Name has the overview of Overcome Fear Through Love. If you note this and absorb what the description says you will see that using Contemplation Magic you could uncover fears that have led to loneliness, make yourself more open to friendship and love, or gain insight into ways to overcome your feelings of solitude. The description of the power is short and sweet, while the power itself has infinite possibilities.

With 72 Sigils of Power, each giving you the power to meditate on your deepest self, and your connection to the universe, as well as manifesting changes in the real world, the number of powers at your disposal is huge! If you're not sure what to do, or how to work with this book, don't worry about getting it right. The magic is so simple and easy, that if you're in any doubt, just try out a word and see what you discover. You're certain to find out something about yourself when you meditate on these Names, and that's the beginning of magic.

Scanning the Letter Shapes

You've followed your intuition and logic to choose the Sigil of Power that is best for your needs, now you scan your eyes over the letters at the same time as thinking or speaking the Words of Power (these are directly derived from Divine Names). While your eyes are going over the letters of the Sigil, you just focus on a particular frame of mind, feeling or intention. We'll look at the feelings in the next chapter. This chapter is here to give you confidence when using this letter-scanning technique.

The idea of letter scanning is that you aren't trying to read the Names or focus on the letters, you move your eyes over them from right to left but only take in the shapes. You don't need to be able to read Hebrew because the sacred shapes are perceived by your soul. If you *are* able to read Hebrew, try and let go of your knowledge and look at the letters as meaningless shapes. You know this is a Name of God so you just trustingly appreciate the shapes, and let them soak through your eyes. Below is a little diagram to remind you to move your eyes from right to left:

You can gently gaze at the sigil, not staring at the details or even focusing your eyes. You should be relaxed.

Feel the letters sink into your consciousness while moving your eyes over their shapes, right to left (indicated by the arrow).

Don't overthink this. You can scan quickly or slowly and it doesn't matter. It doesn't matter if you accidentally read the wrong way for a second, or if you find your eyes settling on one letter. Try to keep your gaze within the circle – that's what it's there for. If your eyes drift outside the circle, bring them back and continue, with a calm state of mind.

You may find that the letters sometimes appear to shimmer, or change to white against a black background. If this happens, don't worry. If it doesn't happen, don't worry. The letter-scanning technique is this simple: you move your eyes over the letters, from right to left. That's it!

This process can take you two minutes or you can go for as long as you want. Being relaxed while scanning the letters is important, so don't worry about whether you're getting it right. So long as you move your eyes over these letter shapes – so long as you see them – you are taking them into your soul.

The magic is brought to life by your intention and by speaking the Words of Power so don't worry about accidentally seeing the Names. It's perfectly OK to look at these Names casually when skimming through the book. It won't do any harm or accidentally trigger the magic.

How to Perform Contemplation Magic

Find a time and place where you can remain peaceful for a few minutes. You should allow at least ten minutes to be available. It's highly possible that the process will be over in one minute. Sometimes you gain insights and explore feelings, and you may want to spend longer, so it's good to make sure the time is available.

You can do this first thing in the morning, right before bed, or whenever you're confident that others will respect your privacy and not disturb you. You can perform this magic while sitting reading the book, so long as the people around you know not to disturb you when you are reading.

Even though there are usually at least two powers listed under each Name, you should only work on one power at a time. Focusing on one power at a time means you're giving the right amount of energy and attention to the working. (You might work on several powers over the course of a day, but for each session, just use one power at a time.)

Let's say you want to find out more about your feelings for your partner, so you've chosen the seventh Name, Acha, and its power called The Connection To Love. Perhaps you've been having doubts about your feelings, and you want to know whether this comes from a real change within you, or perhaps from jealousy, anger or something else that could pass.

You begin the working by acknowledging what state you are in right now. You think about the thing you're going to contemplate. For this working, you would think gently about your love toward your partner. You spend a few moments thinking about how you feel at this exact moment in time. You don't have to give it a name or label or decide whether it's a good or bad feeling and you should not try to change it or manipulate it in any way. Just become aware of what you're feeling. For some workings, you may get in touch with your feelings quickly and easily, and for others, you may need to take your time. Your feelings don't need to be consistent or even understood by you. Just ponder the question that's on your mind and notice how you feel. In this working with Acha, you might feel a little anxious or doubtful about your love. As soon as you've noticed your feelings, move to the next stage.

Scan your eyes over the letter shapes, and verbally or internally, say the Divine Word listed under Contemplation Magic for Acha. For this example, the Word of Power is ACK-AH-AH. (Whatever Name of God you're working with, the Word of Power you need is written beneath the words 'Contemplation Magic', just above the list of powers.)

You continue to scan your eyes over the letter shapes while saying the divine Word of Power, remaining aware of the question that's on your mind. Make room for new thoughts in your mind while staying relaxed, but don't *try* to gain insights or control your thoughts and feelings. All this means is that you allow whatever thoughts and feelings arise to arise.

You are doing three things at once – Letter-scanning, speaking a Word of Power and contemplating a thought or feeling, which might sound demanding but when you give it a try you'll realize it's actually easier than trying to do each step at a time. If you just scan a word, you will find all sorts of thoughts enter your head. If you just try to hold onto a thought or feeling, your mind will drift. If it feels a bit like meditation, that's because it is: scanning, speaking a Name and holding a thought is a form of instant (and highly effective) meditation.

And that's all there is to it. You keep scanning the letters, observing your thoughts and feelings, and you see what happens. In this example, you might think about the love for your partner, and as you do so, you get a better understanding of the reality of your love. Often you will gain an insight that immediately makes you want to ask a new question. Sometimes you will have feelings that you don't yet understand. Sometimes you will obtain immediate wisdom. Often, nothing will happen at all. It may take a few days for the magic to seep through to your consciousness. You may want to perform the magic once, or you may want to come back to the same problem each day, to gain deeper insights. Use your intuition and the magical feedback to help you decide whether you need to continue with the Contemplation Magic. No one else can decide for you.

In Summary, this is the process:

- You choose a Name and Power and a subject you want to contemplate.

- You notice how you feel about this question or thought, in this exact moment.

- As soon as you perceive your current feelings, you begin to scan the letters as instructed in the previous chapter.

- As you scan the letters, you continue to hold the thought, question or subject in your mind.

- You don't force thoughts, but allow them to arise.

- You stop when it feels right to stop. Sometimes you gain immediate insights or wisdom. Sometimes your feelings change. Sometimes nothing happens for a while, and that is OK.

- You repeat if you want, as often as you want. Or you may leave it at that.

Contemplation Magic is about more than meditation on a thought or feeling. You can use it to change your feelings or to release the inner person you believe yourself to be. The process is a little different.

Let's say you want to develop your ability to perceive situations clearly. Perhaps you work in investigation or maybe you're a writer or even a psychologist. If you're pursuing these vocations, we'll assume that you want to develop your ability to perceive people more clearly. You might choose the eighth

Name, Kahet, and the Contemplation power called See Beyond The Obvious. You get the feeling that this power could help you to perceive things more clearly.

The first thing you need to do is think about the power that you want, and how you feel that power is currently lacking in your life. If this aspect of your personality is completely new, you may feel a great sense of lack. While, if you're already expressing this aspect of your personality to some extent, the feeling of lack won't be as strong. Don't fake or force your feeling. It's absolutely enough just to be aware of how you feel about not having this powerfully expressed in your personality. That means that in this working, although the power is called See Beyond The Obvious, you would think about your work and the fact that you can't always perceive things as well as you want to. You notice how this makes you feel. You move onto the next step as soon as you notice what it is that you're feeling.

You start by scanning the letters, as per the letter-scanning technique and you say the Word of Power aloud, or saying it in your mind is fine. For this Name, the Word of Power is KAH-HEH-TAH. You imagine what it would feel like to have this powerfully expressed in your personality while you scan the Name and say the Word of Power. You're not trying to imagine the desired power, but the feeling of joy you would have if your wish came true and you gained that power.

Just let yourself feel glad as you know that you have more of this power in your personality, now. With our perception example, you would feel joyful about your stronger ability to perceive. (If it helps, you could imagine yourself at work, feeling good because you're able to be more perceptive in the ways you wanted to be. If this kind of visualization doesn't work for you, just feel good that you're now more perceptive.)

It's vital that you create some sensation of relief or pleasure at gaining this aspect of personality. Importantly, you don't have to feel the power itself. Don't worry about feeling an improved perception - that feeling would be too abstract and tricky to conjure. Instead, use the strength of your imagination to feel relieved and happy as if your perception is already improved, because it is!

As soon as you get that feeling, you can stop. Feel free to keep going and to repeat this until it's fully engraved in your personality. Sometimes, though, one session will work.

In this example, we looked at improving perception, but there is so much more you can do. Using this aspect of Contemplation Magic you can make yourself calmer, more active, more charismatic, give yourself more compassion, be more resilient, and work on hundreds of other aspects of yourself, bringing out the person you want to be.

If you're not sure what powers you want, or who you want to be, use the first technique described in this chapter, to get a better understanding of yourself, your needs and how you want to change.

How to Perform Results Magic

You can perform this magic anywhere you like, but make sure you have at least five minutes spare, where you will be able to find some peace and remain undisturbed.

If you want ten different results, you *can* work on them all at once, but this magic does require some emotional energy, so be careful not to drain yourself. If you really want to work on ten results, it's probably a good idea to work with one power every hour until all ten are done. This is preferred over trying to work with ten different powers in one sitting. If you can find the patience, it's better to work with just two or three results at any one time. Find out what you really want, and work with that.

At times, you might want to direct a few different powers at one problem. Earlier, for example, we looked at using Sit and Elad to gain charisma. I would recommend this approach if you are using multiple powers on a single problem. You perform the working with one Sigil and then you perform the same working with the next Sigil. It's time-consuming to use too many powers at once, so choose wisely.

For simplicity's sake, we'll use an example in which you only use one power to get one result. I want you to imagine that you are afraid of an upcoming interview, and you know that your fear could ruin your chances of success. Contemplation Magic would work well here for inner change, but for making a more definite change to your fear response you choose to perform Results Magic. We look through the book for something to affect feelings, and fears specifically, and we find the eighth Name, Kahet, has the power To Ease Fears About a Situation under Results Magic. Excellent! You could direct this at your fear of the interview, giving you the confidence to show your abilities.

Notice how you feel about the situation now. In our scary interview scenario, you may notice that you have fear about the interview, and you may have many other negative feelings associated with this fear, such as concern that you won't get the job. Allow all the feelings around this subject to arise, but make sure your ultimate focus is on the one part of this situation you are trying to *change*. In this case, you would bring your focus back to the essential fear of the interview. Holding onto this feeling may be unpleasant, so don't put up with the discomfort. Once you've felt it, you can quickly move onto the next step.

Scan the letter shapes while saying or thinking the Divine Word of Power listed under Results Magic for Kahet. In this scenario, the Word of Power is KAH-HET. (You may have noticed by now that the Word of Power usually appears to be a direct pronunciation of the Name. It's written directly beneath the words 'Results Magic', so you can't miss it.)

While you scan the letters as you say the Divine Name to yourself, you should imagine what it would feel like to have the result that you want. Don't waste imagination stressing about what it would take for this result to happen, just imagine how happy you will be when it does happen!

If you think you've no imagination, it's just not true. We spend all our lives imagining different futures. Ever imagined what it would be like to win the lottery? See! You have plenty of imagination. Even the fear of the interview (that we're using in this example) is a form of imagination. Fear is just an embodiment of an imagined disaster. So it's easy to imagine what it would be like to have something good. But here's the trick. Use your imagination to convince yourself for a moment that it's already happened and that your dream has come true, the result has come to pass and that all is well.

Going back to the job interview, you would imagine feeling a rush of joy – you're walking out of the interview room, delighted that you had no fear. It might take a while to get this feeling. You can stop as soon as you catch the feeling you're after, but keep scanning the Sigil and saying the Word of Power until then.

In Summary, this is the process:

- You choose a Name and Power to bring about the result you want.

- You notice how you feel about whatever result it is that you currently lack.

- You scan the letters in the Sigil as instructed in the previous chapter.

- As you scan the letters, imagine how good you would feel if you got your result.

- Imagine this feeling as though it's already happened.

- You stop as soon as you catch that feeling.

Different results take different lengths of time to manifest, but how do you know what's the right length of time to perform the magic for? If you start this magic one month before your interview, do you keep going until the day of the interview, or when your fear goes away? Neither. You can stop long before the result manifests. Most of the time, you can expect results within days!

It's almost impossible to say exactly how long you should perform the magic for. Sometimes, you might only have three days in which to perform the magic. It's Monday, and your interview is on Wednesday, so you might do it every morning until your interview. But what if you have more time to spare? You can stop after a few days.

I am not going to say stop after three days, or seven days, or eleven days because that will prevent you from feeling your way through this magic. At some point, when performing Results Magic, you will get to the end of the working and you will feel a subtle emotional click, as though everything has started slotting into place. This will give you a sense of trust that the result will come about. At that point you can stop.

What if you never sense this emotional click, or if you have no idea what I'm talking about? Confidently stop after a few days and have trust in the magic, and know that it will work. This is a hundred times more effective than doing it for weeks and weeks hoping you're getting your message through. Remember, you are working with angelic powers and Divine Names – you're always being heard. You don't have to get this exactly right. Expect the result, but never look for it or seek it out, and the result will find you.

Getting the Details Right

You might have a hundred questions about getting the details right. You might want to know what to think, what to feel, which power to use, but please trust me. This is a mystical process, and the previous chapters have given you enough knowledge to get into the magic. It's now time for you to do that. Try the magic, trust it, let it work through your life.

There are a few puzzles that might occupy your mind. Sigil 11 and Sigil 17 are identical, with the same pronunciations. The same is true of Sigil 1 and Sigil 49. How can they work different kinds of magic if they look and sound the same? By tuning your intention to the listed powers, you will access the correct Name and the appropriate powers. It's as simple as that.

If you're not sure how to pronounce the Word of Power, there's a pronunciation guide in the back of the book. That can be useful even if you're saying the words in your mind, rather than out loud.

Now, get to the magic. You have access to hundreds of powers, so stop worrying and start creating.

The 72 Sigils of Power

On the following pages, you will find an overview of each Name, along with its powers, followed by the Sigil.

Please make sure that you've read everything that comes before this page before you jump into performing the magic. It's Ok to flip through and see what powers are available, but it's so important that you have a really good understanding of the technique before you start your working. The instructions are super easy and straightforward so why risk complicating the situation by ignoring them?

This book is not a straightforward book of spells or rituals. You won't find a ritual To Attract More Money or a spell to Bring You a Lover. It's not that kind of book, but you can probably tell that if you delve into the mystical aspects of this magic, you have the ability to attract the changes you want, attracting what you want, and living the life you dream of. At times, the powers will seem obscure. Remember that you may need to meditate on them, spend some time thinking about them and getting to know them. When you read about the power such as An Awareness of Coincidence, you may think it would be easier to do a quick money spell. It would be easier, but don't be put off by the subtle nature of this book. This magic works on such a deep level that if you give it your attention and perception, it will reward you.

If you're sure that you're all read-up and ready to go, then I invite you to start your magical working with the 72 Sigils of Power.

1. Vehu

Manifestation and Strength

ו הו ו

This Name is concerned with universal unity, and the perception that our strength in the material world can lead to the greatest spiritual growth, while our spiritual growth can lead to great material strength.

Contemplation Magic

VAH-HEH-VAH

Strength and willpower.

Knowledge of what we can manifest.

Unraveling the mystery of how you came to be where you are.

Results Magic

VEH-WHO

To obtain strength when facing a difficult situation.

To manifest a desire.

2. Yeli

Overcome Fear Through Love

י ל י

This Name can guide you to connect with the power of love, to overcome fear. It can guide you to be at ease with yourself, to overcome blockages and loneliness. When you feel that your life has stagnated, this Name can recover the joy you once felt. Fears can be conquered through the power of love.

Contemplation Magic

YAW-LAH-YAW

Fear of love or fear of loneliness.

The feeling of being stuck.

The sense of being alone.

Results Magic

YELL-EE

To overcome fear through love.

To recover joy.

3. Sit

The Flow of Personality

ס י ט

This Name is concerned with the ebb and flow of your personality. You are not the same person you were ten years ago, so what changes and what is really you? This Name can guide you to uncover and explore the ripples and currents of yourself.

Contemplation Magic

SAH-YAW-TEH

The depths of personality.

The potential for change.

Results Magic

SEET

To improve a personality trait.

To take on a new personality trait.

4. Elem

Recovery

עלם

This Name can aid your recovery from emotional pain and bitterness. If your heart is harmed, it needs to be opened to let in the healing light. This Name will open your heart to the light of recovery.

Contemplation Magic

AHLAH-MEH

The feelings beneath feelings.

The source of pain.

The people you forgive.

Results Magic

ELL-EM

To ease emotional pain and anxiety.

To recover from bitterness.

עלם

5. Mahash

Healing and Soulwork

מ הׁ שׁ

The Name Mahash gives you direct access to the depths of your soul, to provide healing or to clarify your doubts and fears. When you have been attacked, glimpsing your soul can aid your recovery. When your soul feels troubled, a clear sight of it can ease your fears, doubts, and worries.

Contemplation Magic

MEH-HEH-SHE

The reaction to pain.

Yearning for the soul.

Results Magic

MAH-HAHSH

To heal after a physical attack.

To recover fully when an illness has already passed.

To ease a troubled soul.

6. Lelah

The Body of Peace

ללה

Concerned with silence, peace and the body, this Name can bring your attention to the calm beauty of your physical self, your inner peace, and the messages in your dreams. The Name is also used to relieve anxiety that manifests in the body.

Contemplation Magic

LAH-LAH-HEH

The peace of silence.

The calm of the flesh.

The wisdom of dreams.

Results Magic

LEH-LAH

To ease anxiety felt in the body.

7. Acha

Understand Connections

אבא

Acha can help you to see how you relate to other people and things. Some connections may be vital to your purpose, while others should be released from your grasp. The Name will enable you to see what you need, what you can release, and will help you to let go of the burdens you no longer require.

Contemplation Magic

ACK-AH-AH

The connection to people.

The connection to love.

The connection to hope.

The connection to fear.

Results Magic

ACH-AH

To let go of fear.

To release unwanted attachment.

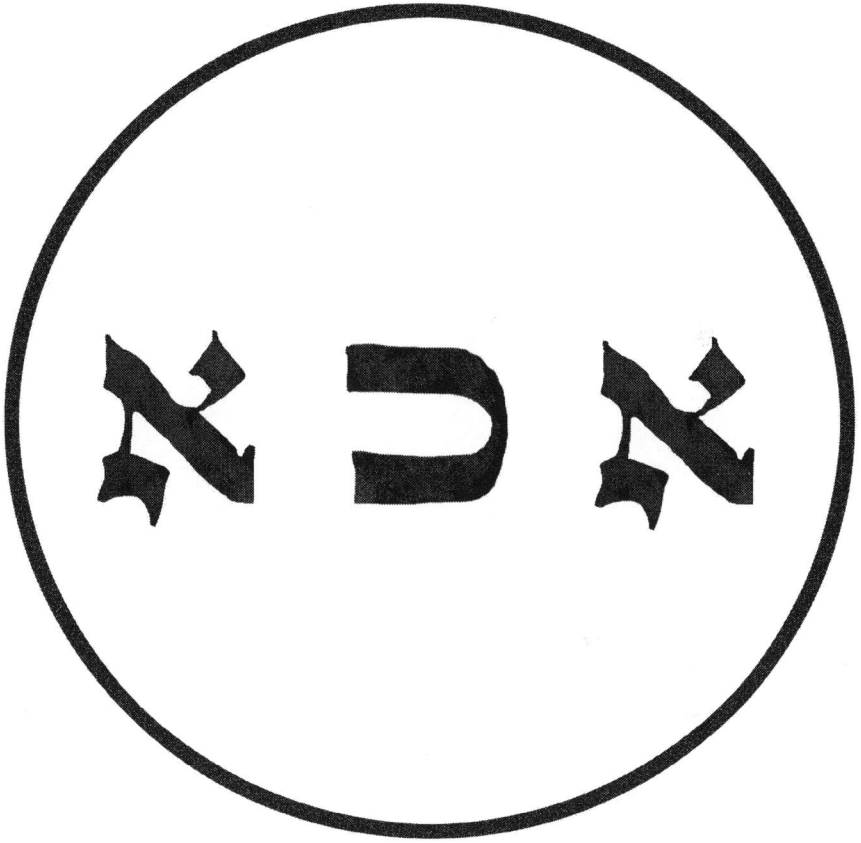

8. Kahet

To Find Light in the Dark

כ ה ה ת

This Name gives you the ability to see beyond the obvious darkness of your life and find what is good in any time or place. The Name can free you from negative influence and ease your fears.

Contemplation Magic

KAH-HEH-TAH

Feel the darkness fully, and within it find light.

See beyond the obvious.

Results Magic

KAH-HET

To remove the negative influence of other people.

To ease fears about a situation.

9. Hezi

Messages and Truth

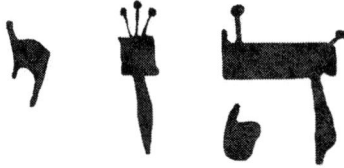

אִבַּהּ

Angels are messengers, and this Name gives you access to angelic communication. When you seek truth or wish to detect the meaning behind lies, you can use this Name. It can help you to communicate your truth through words and art.

Contemplation Magic

HEH-ZAH-YAW

The truth of communication.

The wisdom of words.

The weight of lies.

Results Magic

HEH-ZEE

To get your message across.

To convey truth through art.

10. Elad

Moments of Joy

אֵלָד

When you feel disconnected from enjoying the present moment, use this Name. It can help you to see the present moment with greater clarity, and understand the joy that is an undercurrent in your life.

Contemplation Magic

AHLAH-DAH

The clarity of the present.

The reality of joy.

Results Magic

ELL-AHD

To find joy in the present moment.

To increase personal charisma.

אלד

11. Lav

The Bonds of Connection

לאו

Lav is a Name that is concerned with your relationships to friends, enemies, and strangers. By connecting with this Name, you can discover the talents that can bring you popularity, but also see genuine friendship, and understand why you fear enemies and why they fear you.

Contemplation Magic

LAH-AHVAH

The bonds of friendship.

The fear of enemies.

Results Magic

LAHV

To discover talents.

To banish evil intentions.

12. Haha

Unconditional Love

Haha is a Name concerned with unconditional love. The love we experience in human relationships is often conditional. It depends on attractions, affinity, and many other factors. But what lies beneath the love that never leaves us can be accessed through this Sigil.

Contemplation Magic

HEH-HEH-AH

The source of love.

The approach of love.

The acceptance of love.

Results Magic

HAH-AH

To bring love where there is hatred.

To understand the mystery of attraction.

65

13. Yezel

Strength and Inspiration

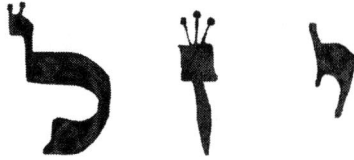

ל ז י

With Yezel you have access to strength and inspiration. Although strength may seem like force, and inspiration may seem like the passive act of receiving, strength is more powerful when inspired, and inspiration is most effective when followed through with strength.

Contemplation Magic

YAW-ZAH-LAH

The strength of many within one.

The strength to overcome the past.

Results Magic

YEH-ZELL

To be inspired.

To complete a work of art.

To repel those who criticize.

14. Mebah

Peace

מ ב ל ה

Associated with peace, Mebah can bring temporary peace to conflict, or guide you to find continuing peace despite the outer circumstances. The Name can connect you to your innate sense of goodness, giving you a sense of where you really belong in the world.

Contemplation Magic

MEH-BEH-HEH

The peace of understanding.

The sense of goodness.

Results Magic

MEB-AH

To know where you belong.

To find peace.

15. Hari

Good Judgment

י ר הֹ

With the good judgment of the Name Hari, you have the power to access understanding and knowledge, to make good decisions or get others to support your decisions, and judge you in a favorable light.

Contemplation Magic

HEH-REH-YAW

The calm of good judgment.

The light of understanding.

Results Magic

HAH-REE

To make long-term plans.

To make a big decision.

To make a decision go your way.

To get others to follow your commands.

16. Hakem

Dignity

הקם

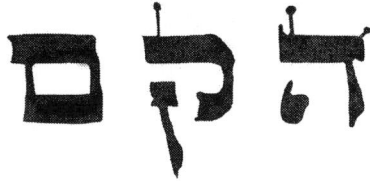

With the Name Hakem you can connect to your innate sense of
dignity. With your dignity intact you can get a better sense of
your inner self, and you can remove the social harm done by
others.

Contemplation Magic

HEH-KAW-MEH

The sense of dignity.

Results Magic

HAH-KEM

To recover from criticism.

To heal sadness after parting.

17. Lav

Invention

לאֵ ו

The Name Lav can be used to connect to the powers of invention, discovering your own sources of inspiration. It can help you to understand art, music and all kinds of design, as well as inspiring your creative work. For musicians, it helps you create melodies that communicate honest messages.

Contemplation Magic

LAH-AHVAH

The depth of art.

The creation of music.

The secrets of invention.

Results Magic

LAHV

To be inspired by true will.

To make music with a message.

18. Keli

Satisfaction and Safety

כלי

Keli is a Name that can enable you to feel satisfaction and appreciation for what you have, as well as bringing you more of the things you need to feel appreciation and satisfaction. It is a powerful Name to use against enemies.

Contemplation Magic

KAH-LAH-YAW

The sense of satisfaction.

The connection to appreciation.

The strength to ignore enemies.

Results Magic

KEH-LEE

To repel attackers.

To withstand the ill will of an enemy.

19. Lov

Love and Dreams

לוו

Lov can help you fulfill dreams when they come from a place of love. The Name can draw love to you, and help you understand and appreciate the Divine love that moves through you.

Contemplation Magic

LAH-VAH-VAH

The expression of love.

A connection to the life force.

A sense of divinity.

The meaning of dreams.

Results Magic

LAWV

To fulfill a dream.

To attract the love of one you care for.

20. Pahal

Recover The Self

פהל

The Name Pahal gives you access to parts of yourself that are hidden, such as inner dreams and hopes. This connection enables you to recover yourself, giving up addictions and bad habits, or being resolute in the face of challenges.

Contemplation Magic

PEH-HEH-LAH

Knowledge of yourself.

Hidden dreams.

Results Magic

PAH-HAHL

To be resolute.

To recover the lost self.

To remove unwanted habits.

21. Nelach

Reverse The Fall

נֵלַךְ

With the power of the Name Nelach you can understand your current situation in terms of luck or fortune, and when it is declining, reverse it. The Name can help you to gain strength when unwell, see the reality of apparent evil, and even stir up love.

Contemplation Magic

NOO-LAH-KAH

The reversal of fortune.

Perspective in the face of evil.

Strength from within sickness.

Results Magic

NEH-LACH

To reverse bad luck.

To stir love.

נכר

22. Yeyay

Remove The Unwanted

ה ה ה

The Name Yeyay gives you the ability to overcome the unwanted influence of others in your life, especially when that influence harms you. Unwanted friends will no longer influence you or get in your way.

Contemplation Magic

YAW-YAW-YAW

Overcome the influence of others.

The reaction to negativity.

The pleasure of solitude.

Results Magic

YEH-YAY

To remove unwanted friends.

To clear negative influences.

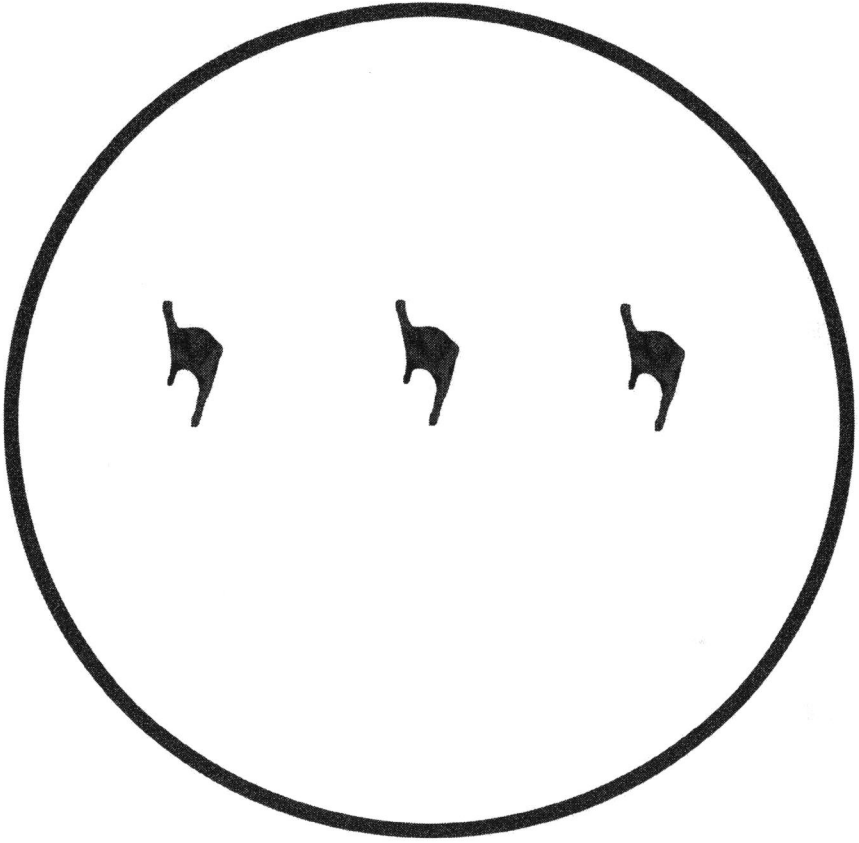

23. Melah

Protection in Darkness

מלה

With Melah you can access the power of clear thought and a sense of safety, even when the world around you appears to be cloaked in darkness and confusion.

Contemplation Magic

MEH-LAH-HEH

The clarity of thought.

A sense of joy beneath apprehension.

Results Magic

MEH-LAH

To think clearly when times are confusing.

To be protected when the situation is dangerous.

24. Chaho

The Reality of Magic

וֹ הֵ חַ

The Name Chaho is connected to your personal magic, your ability to accept and understand magic, and to create change in the world in accordance with your will. The Name can also give you insight into jealousy, and help others to protect you.

Contemplation Magic

CHEH-HEH-VAH

The surety of magic.

Understanding of jealousy.

Results Magic

CHAH-HAW

To connect with magic.

To create a new reality.

To be made safe by others.

25. Netah

Justice and Restraint

נְתָה

The powerful Name Netah is concerned with justice, and can be used to uncover lies, silence liars, and restrain others from causing harm. The underlying sense of justice associated with this Name can cause a cruel enemy to dread you, and feel regret for causing you harm.

Contemplation Magic

NOO-TAH-HEH

The arrival of justice.

Seeing truth behind lies.

Results Magic

NET-AH

To silence liars.

To prevent others from causing you harm

To cause your enemy to dread you.

26. Haah

Finding Your Way

א א ה

Haah is a Name that can remove the chaos from your life, and give you the clarity to decide on the best pathway to follow. It is a Name that offers guidance when you are lost.

Contemplation Magic

HEH-AH-AH

Unraveling the mystery of where you are going.

Finding your true path in any situation.

Results Magic

HAH-AH

To find a definite answer.

To decide upon the best course of action.

27. Yeret

The Essence of Change

ת ר י י

With the Name Yeret you can gain deep insight into the vows and promises you have made, including those you have forgotten, giving you an understanding of why you may have stagnated. You can be released from vows, understand how best to bring about change, and attract abundance where there is already some growth.

Contemplation Magic

YAW-REH-TAH

An understanding of promises and vows.

Release from a vow.

Understanding how to make changes.

Results Magic

YEH-RET

To increase abundance in any area of life.

To sense your innate life force.

28. Shaah

Thriving

שׁ אָ הִ

The Name Shaah is about the transformation of sparks into flame and the energy of a full life. From tiny sparks come great flames. The Name is associated with the beginning of a new venture, and rapid growth, as well as the rush of passion, and the ability to thrive.

Contemplation Magic

SHE-AH-EH

The beginning of a venture.

The fire of passion.

A sense of how you can live fully.

Results Magic

SHAH-AH

To recover from illness and thrive.

To increase personal energy.

To dedicate yourself to a new venture.

29. Riyi

Ending Hostility

רִ יִ יִ

No matter how good your intentions, you may be held back by the hostility of others. The Name Riyi can help attract the acceptance of others and even their kindness. If others are holding you back, through hostility and jealousy, this Name can arrest their negative influence.

Contemplation Magic

REH-YAW-YAW

The end of hostility.

The feeling of being accepted.

Results Magic

REE-YEE

To end conflict.

To remove blockages caused by those who thwart you.

To manifest desires through the kindness of others.

30. Om

Secret Knowledge

אום

Knowledge is power, and the Name Om can uncover many kinds of secret knowledge, from the mystical to the practical. Where something is hidden from you, or hidden because you are unable to see it, this Name can guide you to truth.

Contemplation Magic

AHVAH-MEH

The discovery of secret knowledge.

Guidance through the discovery of hidden truth.

Results Magic

AWM

To understand your true needs.

To discover potent secrets about yourself.

To discover the secrets that others hide.

31. Lekav

Good Understanding

לְכָב

The Name Lekav brings understanding, especially when the neglect of others causes confusion. If you are bewildered by the harm being caused to you, this Name can bring understanding and remove spite from relationships.

Contemplation Magic

LAH-KAH-BEH

The sense of mercy.

Bringing sense where there is confusion.

Easing torment where there is confusion.

Results Magic

LEH-KAV

To end wickedness.

To remove spite.

To increase trust in a relationship.

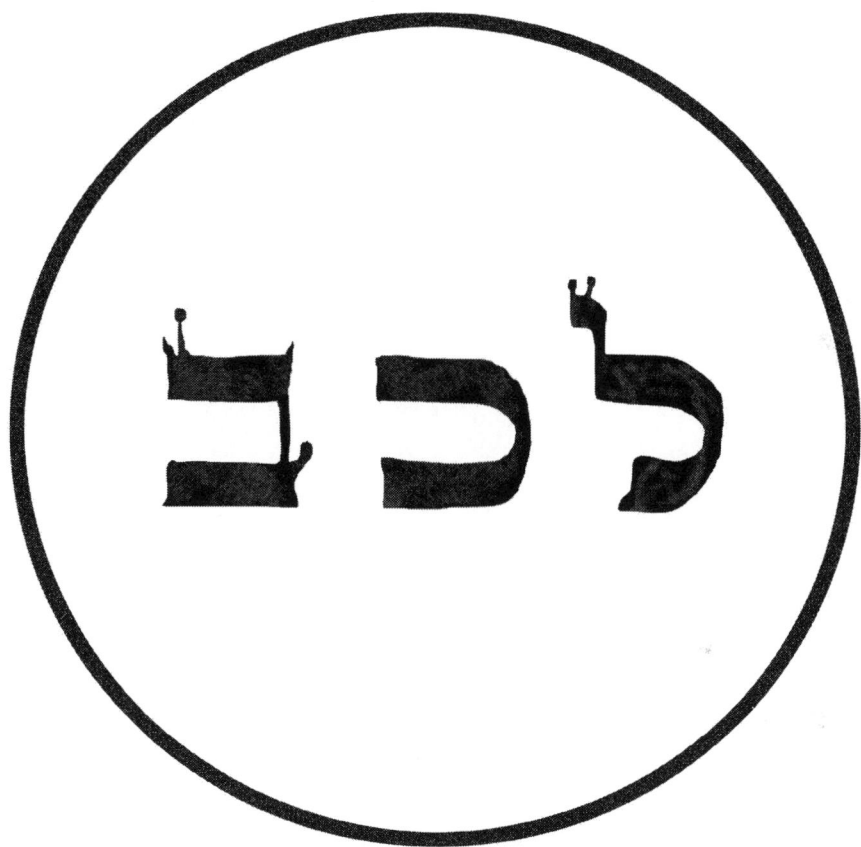

32. Vesher

Memory and Knowledge

ו שׂ ר

The Name Vesher is associated with the power of recall and will assist you in improving your memory and learning new tasks. It will not uncover the past but can make new knowledge sink into the depths of your being.

Contemplation Magic

VAH-SHE-REH

The acceptance of new knowledge.

Your connection to memory.

Results Magic

VEH-SHAR

To improve memory.

To understand a new subject.

To speak clearly about a subject.

33. Yichu

Reaction

וּ חֻ יִ

The Name Yichu is concerned with your reactions to others, and the way others may oppress you. This Name can enlighten you and deliver you from oppression while easing your reactive compulsions.

Contemplation Magic

YAW-CHEH-VAH

Understanding the nature of reaction.

The sense of subjugation.

Results Magic

YEE-CHOO

To overcome reactions.

To ease compulsion.

To be rescued from oppression.

34. Lahach

Letting Go

לַהַח

We are so concerned with getting what we want that it's easy to forget that letting go of desire is the best way to achieve a desire. The Name Lahach can help you let go of desire, make you focus on giving, and releases you from unwanted attachments.

Contemplation Magic

LAH-HEH-CHEH

The ease of letting go.

The ease of giving.

Results Magic

LUH-HACH

To let go of desire.

To let go of unwanted attachments.

35. Kevek

Sharing Love

כ ו ק

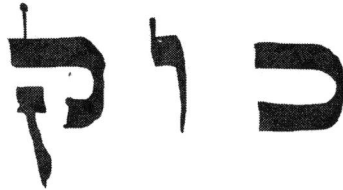

The Name Kevek can connect you to the love you carry within you, helping you bring peace to your family, or offering strength and encouragement to those who need it most.

Contemplation Magic

KAH-VAH-KAW

Sharing your love.

Connecting to those who need your love.

The strength of peace within family.

Results Magic

KEH-VEK

To protect the meek.

To encourage those who are at a loss.

36. Menad

Removing Fear

מנד

The Name Menad is associated with fear, and enables you to conquer fear, and transforms fears into memories that can no longer control you. The Name can also dazzle an enemy with your courage and inner light so that they lose the will to harm you.

Contemplation Magic

MEH-NOO-DAH

Feeling courage in the present.

The release of fear.

Results Magic

MEH-NAD

To conquer fear.

To put fears in your past.

To blind an enemy with light.

113

37. Ani

Perspective

אֲנִי

The Name Ani can give you perspective on who you really are and your place in the world. It can make problems seem small, reveal your potential, show you the value of your soul and unravel the meaning of your life.

Contemplation Magic

AH-NOO-YAW

The purpose of life.

Problems in perspective.

The importance of self.

Results Magic

AH-KNEE

To render problems insignificant.

To see your potential.

38. Chaam

Sharing The Self

מ ע ח

To receive through magic, you need to give and share through magic. With the Name Chaam you can share yourself, and give your love and wisdom to others.

Contemplation Magic

CHEH-AH-MEH

Unleashing your truth.

Releasing your love.

Results Magic

CHAH-AHM

To convey wisdom.

To be known by others.

39. Reho

Transformation

ר הֹ עְ

The Name Reho is all about transformation. With this Name you can take evil thoughts and negative feelings, and transform them to the good and positive, or bring relief when there is emotional anguish.

Contemplation Magic

REH-HEH-AH

Removing evil thoughts.

The transformation of bad to good.

Peace during troubled times.

Results Magic

REH-HAW

To transform evil into good.

To change emotional pain to relief.

40. Yeyiz

Pure Silence

In every moment we are moving through time, but every moment is a fragment of stillness. The Name Yeyiz draws these fragments together, to reveal silence. When all is still, you may hear yourself.

Contemplation Magic

YAW-YAW-ZAH

The silence of the moment.

Peace within chaos.

Results Magic

YEH-YIZ

To find stillness.

To create without distraction.

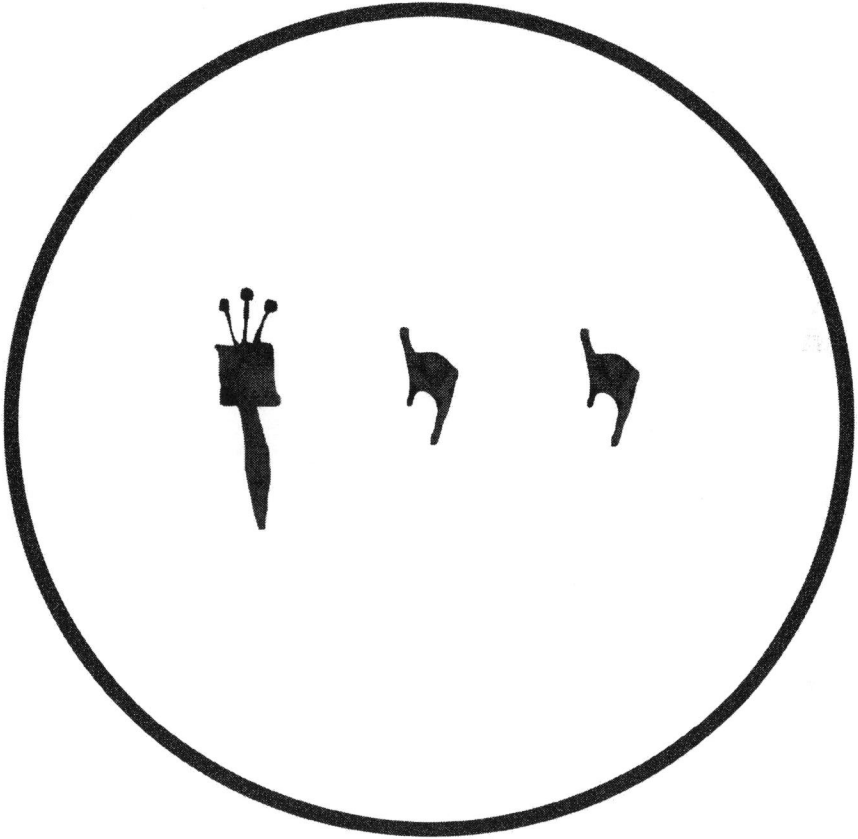

41. Hahah

Open to Sound

ה ה ה

With the power of the Name Hahah you can open yourself to the sounds that surround you while gaining a deeper sense of your soul. When you are receptive to others and aware of your surroundings, you can be present, clear and forgiving of yourself.

Contemplation Magic

HEH-HEH-HEH

The peace of your soul.

An opening to sound.

Results Magic

HAH-HAH-AH

To forgive yourself.

To be fully present.

To hear others clearly.

42. Mich

Collective Wisdom

מ י ך

With the power of the Name Mich, you can connect yourself with groups of people. Politicians, workers, and managers need to contribute to the group, and receive wisdom from the group.

Contemplation Magic

MEH-YAW-KAH

The connection to a group.

Understand your influence over a group.

Receive wisdom from a collective.

Results Magic

MEECH

To influence a group of people.

To gather people to you.

43. Veval

Spirit in The World

וול

If we think of matter as base, and spirit as lofty, we lose out on the spiritual growth that occurs when we manifest our physical desires. Through the Name Veval, you become aware of your soul in the world. It interacts with the world at all times, and this gives us the power to create.

Contemplation Magic

VAH-VAH-LAH

Knowledge of your soul's expression.

The insight gained from manifestation.

The good of creating art for others.

Results Magic

VEH-VAHL

To be known as a creator.

To be seen as powerful.

44. Yelah

The Flow of Love

יְלָה

A river is always moving but never goes away while there is water to feed it. The Name Yelah connects you to a flow of love that does not end, never leaves, but that is always undergoing change.

Contemplation Magic

YAW-LAH-HEH

The maturing of love.

Reconnecting with love.

Results Magic

YEH-LAH

To convey love to others.

To enrich love within a relationship.

45. Sehahl

Prosperity

סאל

Prosperity is not about owning things or earning money, but being open to receive. When you are able to receive, you barely need to attract anything, and you will receive everything.

Contemplation Magic

SEE-AHLAH

The sense of providence.

Appreciation of beauty.

The certainty of prosperity.

Results Magic

SEH-AHL

To become open to prosperity.

To receive without guilt.

סאל

46. Ari

Subtle Plans

עֲ רִ י

With the Name Ari you can plan positive actions for your future without causing harm, without being seen, and without straying from your path. From this secret place, you can do much good and attract great wealth.

Contemplation Magic

ARE-YAW

Creation with compassion.

The wealth of sharing.

A sense of the future.

Results Magic

AH-REE

To plan for success.

To keep plans concealed.

47. Eshal

Commanding Presence

עֶ שֶׁ לִ

With the Name Eshal, you can access Divine authority, and command with the presence of a great leader. Spirits will cooperate, and the people who are willfully under your command will be awed by your splendor.

Contemplation Magic

AH-SHE-LAH

A sense of leadership.

The defense of your realm.

The power to command spirits.

Results Magic

ESH-AHL

To make others stand in awe of you.

To command with great leadership.

48. Mih

The Bridge of Mercy

מ י ה

With the Name Mih you touch the bridge that leads to Divine mercy, and from this power, you can feel mercy for others, understand the needs of the many, obtain a sense of forgiveness, or unite those who are apart.

Contemplation Magic

MEH-YAW-HEH

A connection to the sense of mercy.

Insight into the mystery of the greater good.

Results Magic

ME-AH

To be forgiven.

To unite those who have quarreled.

To unite disparate groups to a common good.

49. Vehu

The Clear Heart

וֵהוּ

With a good heart, you are clear to follow your chosen path and manifest the life you want to lead. With the Name Vehu, you can clarify your heart, bring light to the darkness and dwell in the pleasure of the moment. (Although this appears identical to the first Name and sigil out of the seventy-two, it is considered to be a different Name, with different powers.)

Contemplation Magic

VAH-HEH-VAH

The clarity of a good heart.

Enjoyment of the infinite present.

Results Magic

VEH-WHO

To bring light to a darkened heart.

To dispel confusion.

50. Dani

The Light of Prosperity

ד נ י

To achieve a state of prosperity, you release sadness and allow success to be ongoing. You are not looking for one quick win to deliver you from anguish, but to release anguish so that you can journey continually through prosperity.

Contemplation Magic

DAH-NOO-YAW

The light that guides through prosperity.

The release of sadness.

The ease when anguish leaves.

Results Magic

DAH-KNEE

To remove anxiety and sadness.

To experience prosperity in the present moment.

To remove guilt about money.

51. Hachash

Truth

הֵ וֵ שׁ

The Truth may set you free, but it takes courage to use the Name Hachash to see the truth that lies beneath your feelings. Is your love real, or based on fear? In the depths of this Name you experience truthful insights, free of deception and confusion that may be brought on by fear and habit.

Contemplation Magic

HEH-CHEH-SHE

Observe the truth behind your feelings.

Thought without self-deception.

Feelings without chaotic thought.

Results Magic

HACH-AHSH

To know the truth about yourself.

To understand the true potential of a relationship.

To see those you love as they truly are.

52. Omem

Bending Time

עמם

Time can be shifted with the power of the Name Omem. When time is short, it can be made longer. When change is slow to come, it can be pulled closer.

Contemplation Magic

AH-MEH-MEH

The strengthening of memory.

Moving faster without fatigue.

Understanding more in less time.

Results Magic

AWM-EM

To achieve much in a short time.

To bring about rapid change.

145

53. Nena

Friendship

אנ ננ

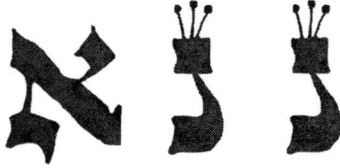

Unless tended well, friendships fail and fall into bitterness and anger. With the Name Nena, you can charge your friendships with the authentic power of unconditional love. The offer of yourself brings people who love you as you are.

Contemplation Magic

NOO-NOO-AH

The sense of being authentic around friends.

Honesty in friendship.

Results Magic

NEH-NAH

To make friendship firm.

To draw new friends to your light.

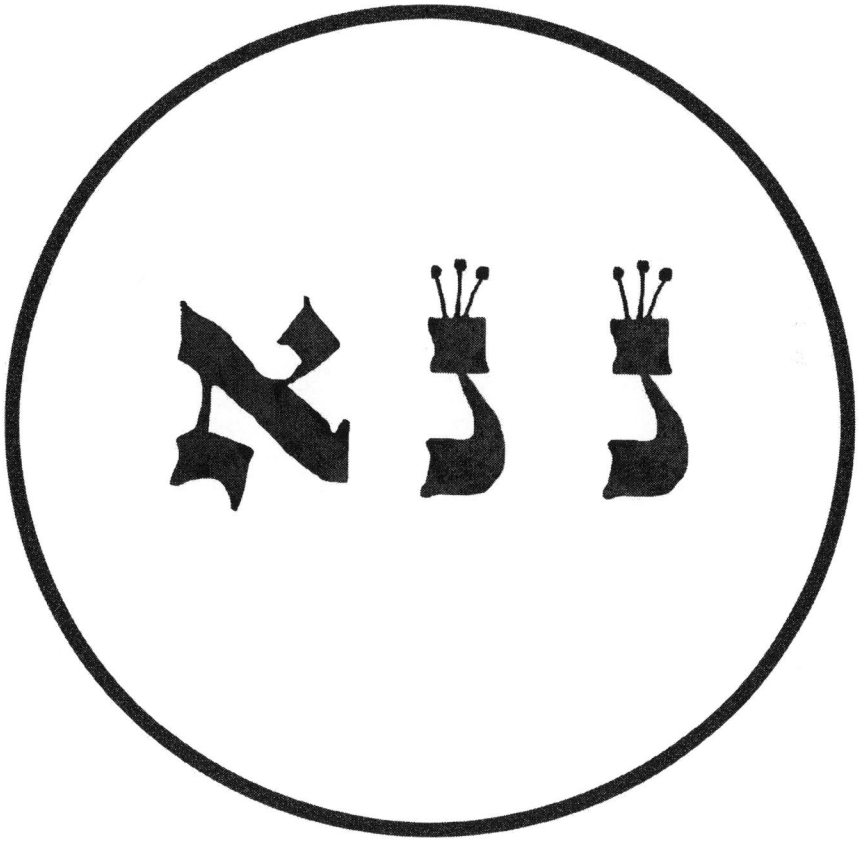

54. Nit

Fruition

נִית

Using the Name Nit, you can make the projects you love come to fruition. When everything is in place, this is the Name that moves you from concepts and plans to production.

Contemplation Magic

NOO-YAW-TAH

The courage of creation.

The sense of commitment to a task.

Results Magic

NEET

To make a vision real.

To convey your produce to others.

55. Mivah

Talent

מבּה

You may be capable of more than you believe. Whatever talents you have, there may be more hidden away by fear and distraction. The Name Mivah can connect you to your talents, and help you see where your passion can take you.

Contemplation Magic

MEH-BEH-HEH

Perception of your own true talents.

The passion of creation.

Results Magic

ME-VAH

To be recognized for your creations.

To connect with the highest potential of your talent.

151

56. Poi

Esteem

פ ו י

When you are too proud, you are unlikely to be well loved, but you need a good sense of self-esteem in order to enjoy the reward of love. With the Name Poi you can lift your esteem so that you are adored for the creations you bring to the world.

Contemplation Magic

PEH-VAH-YAW

A comfortable sense of self.

Understanding the worth of your talent.

Results Magic

PAW-EE

To be loved for your work.

To remove doubts about your talent.

153

57. Nemem

Growth

נ מ ם

When you are in a state of creation, the Name Nemem will help you to maintain the creation, and let your work flourish. Whether you seek ideas, profit or production, this Name can bring growth to that which is already in place.

Contemplation Magic

NOO-MEH-MEH

The state of expansion and growth.

Results Magic

NEM-EM

To make a project flourish.

To receive deeper inspiration as your project progresses.

58. Yeyil

Originality

To thrive you will need to come up with new ideas, new ways of working, and new ways of thinking and feeling. Originality is a power that can be accessed through the Name Yeyil.

Contemplation Magic

YAW-LAH-LAH

Being open to new ideas.

Letting go of old ways.

Results Magic

YEH-YEEL

To find a new solution to an old problem.

To generate ideas.

To think in an original way.

59. Harach

Movement into The Light

 הֲ רַ וֹ חַ

When your feelings are clouded or stained, the Name Harach can move you into a lighter place. When you move from one place to another, you are not the same person in a different place, but a new moment of reality. Let this Name move you to a place where you a free of the darkness.

Contemplation Magic

HEH-REH-CHEH

The acceptance of a lighter mood.

The first glimmer of hope.

A state of happiness.

Results Magic

HAH-RAHCH

To dispel dark moods.

To move on from emotional pain.

To feel relief, regardless of circumstance.

60. Metzer

Safety in A Storm

מ צ ר

When the world around you is in turmoil, stand in the eye of the storm and remain there until the fury has eased. With the Name Metzer, you can find peace when there is chaos, conflict, criticism and slander. You will be left strong, when all around you have been weakened by argument.

Contemplation Magic

MEH-TZAH-REH

The knowledge that every storm will pass.

Calm strength and patience.

Results Magic

METZUR

To deflect criticism.

To be unmoved by slander.

To remain calm in the middle of chaos.

61. Umab

Wise Decisions

וּמַבּ

Wisdom is of no use if it is not acted on, and to act on wisdom, you need to make a decision. The Name Umab will prevent you from dithering and wondering, and will enable you to make wise decisions that others will see as wise.

Contemplation Magic

VAH-MEH-BEH

Moving from thought to decision.

The call of intuition.

Results Magic

OOM-AHB

To make a good decision.

To be seen as wise.

ומב

62. Yahah

Ruling With Honor

הָהָה‎

The Name Yahah can bring you the confidence of acting as a great ruler. When you feel the sense of being a great ruler, you do not need to force, cajole or intimidate those around you. Your words will compel them to do what you ask because they respect you.

Contemplation Magic

YAW-HEH-HEH

The authority of a ruler.

The wisdom to do what helps you and those around you.

Results Magic

YAH-HAH

To be respected.

To receive honors and awards.

To be obeyed without resistance.

63. Anu

Teaching

נ ט ׳ ן

When we teach, we learn, and when we learn we instruct our teachers. With the Name Anu you can attract the teachers you need, and pass on your knowledge to others. Teaching is not about telling, but about instructing one another to be more open to ideas, and in that state, we all learn what we most need to learn.

Contemplation Magic

AH-NOO-VAH

The acceptance of wisdom.

The release of knowledge.

Results Magic

AH-NOO

To find a great teacher.

To pass on your wisdom.

64. Machi

Welcome Messages

מ חִ י

You have messages that you want to convey, and when you convey them with passion, people perceive that the message is a part of you. When you write, create or communicate, the Name Machi puts the light of truth in your messages, making it easy for others to hear you and know you.

Contemplation Magic

MEH-CHEH-YAW

Communicating from your soul.

Knowing what you want to say.

Results Magic

MAH-CHEE

To become more popular.

To be liked for what you say, write or create.

65. Dameb

The Pleasure of Success

רֶמֶב

When you strive for success, you remain in a state of struggle. Success comes in the moment that you enjoy your work, and when the act of working and creating is more important than the reward. The Name Dameb can immerse you in this sense of gratitude for the success you already enjoy, and thus brings more success.

Contemplation Magic

DAH-MEH-BEH

The success within you.

The pleasure of work.

Understanding your contribution to the world.

Results Magic

DAH-MEB

To become at one with success to attract success.

To experience true gratitude.

66. Menak

Forgiveness

מנק

Your desire for revenge can be your enemy's greatest weapon, because it weakens and obsesses you, without your enemy having to lift a finger. When you have served justice, release yourself from the need for revenge with the Name Menak, and you achieve a true victory.

Contemplation Magic

MEH-NOO-KAW

The sense of forgiveness.

Replacing anger with apathy.

The easing of malice.

Results Magic

MEH-NAHK

To let go of enmity and hatred.

To forgive and let go of the need for revenge.

67. Iyah

Breakthrough

עִ י אַ

When you resist change, you need a breakthrough. The Name Iyah can open you to change by removing your resistance, enabling the power of all your magic to break through into your reality.

Contemplation Magic

AH-YAW-AH

Welcoming transformation.

Accepting the discomfort of change.

Understanding the need for change.

Results Magic

EE-AH

To remove mental blockages.

To remove resistance to change.

68. Chavu

Recovery

חבו

When you have begun to recover from emotional pain, illness or despair, the Name Chavu will support you, protect you, and make your recovery sound and ongoing.

Contemplation Magic

CHEH-BEH-VAH

The calm of recovery.

The recovery of self.

Results Magic

CHAH-VOO

To maintain recovery.

To return to full health.

69. Raah

Belonging

רָאֶה

Move on from isolation, and find a way to thrive within a group, through the power of the Name Raah. With a sense of belonging, you can find out where you should be going, where you belong, and where you will be at home.

Contemplation Magic

REH-AH-HEH

The sense of belonging.

Knowing how you connect with others.

Knowing when to lead and when to follow.

Results Magic

RAH-AH

To discover where you belong.

To find new directions when you feel stuck.

To find a family beyond your family.

70. Yabam

Stimulate Coincidence

םב ֿי

Magic works through change, and change is made magical through coincidence. Open the way for coincidence to work in your life, and become aware of the synchronicities that are triggered by your magic. Every time you notice coincidence, you empower your magic.

Contemplation Magic

YAW-BEH-MEH

An awareness of coincidence.

The reassurance of synchronicity.

Results Magic

YAH-BAHM

To stimulate coincidence.

To see patterns in the events of your life.

To make your reality more malleable.

71. Hayi

Awareness

הִיִ

With the Name Hayi, you can extend your awareness beyond yourself, to other people, and to the future. Fall into the present moment completely, and from there, see the thoughts of others, and futures that may come.

Contemplation Magic

HEH-YAW-YAW

A sense of the future.

Greater perception of the present moment.

Results Magic

HAH-YEE

To increase awareness of the self.

To increase awareness of the thoughts of others.

To perceive the future.

72. Mum

Collapse of Structure

מ ו ם

With destruction comes renewal. In order to create anew, we must collapse that which has gone before or tumble the structures that work against us. Within and without, there is much that can be destroyed to make way for the new.

Contemplation Magic

MEH-VAH-MEH

The end of old ways.

Knowledge of what must be destroyed.

A cleansing of the soul.

Results Magic

MOOM

To bring about destruction.

To remove old ways.

Appendix 1. The Source of The 72 Names

I like to know where the inspiration for magical names and numbers comes from and so I'd like to share with you from where The Names of God are derived. They are encoded in three Biblical verses: Exodus 14: 19-21 which is written in a special way, and I can briefly explain how.

The first verse is written from right to left, as is normal for Hebrew. The second verse is written directly below this, but this time from left to right. The final verse is again written from right to left. This gives you 72 columns of three letters. These are the 72 Names of God. Magical, isn't it!

Exactly why you would work with the text in this way, and why 72 is such an important mystical number, would take a whole book to explain. Many have tried, and you will find there are references to these Names in ancient texts such as *Shorshei Ha-Shemot*. But investigating theory is not the point of this book. If you want to research, there's a lot of fascinating info, but also a lot of myth and fantasy. Spend a few hours *working* with the Names and you'll learn all you need to know.

Appendix 2: Pronunciation Guide

The following pronunciation guide was provided by Damon Brand, with only a few additions of my own, and I'm eternally grateful for his hard work.

Pronunciation does not have to be accurate. It is better to be relaxed about the sounds than to aim for perfection. But even when you are saying the words inside your head, getting it 'almost right' is better than a wild guess.

The only sound that presents a challenge is CH, as in the Name Acha (ACH-AH). The CH is not the sound you find in *choose* or *cheese*. If you know the Scottish word *Loch*, or the German word *Achtung*, that's the CH sound you're aiming for. Search YouTube or similar sites for the pronunciation of these words (preferably by Scottish and German speakers respectively), and you'll know how to get it right.

If you simply can't get that CH to sound right, then use the K sound when you see CH. So for ACH-AH, you would say AK-AH. This is not ideal, but it will still work.

The English word *ah* is often used for reference. Given that this word is pronounced in many different ways, here is some clarification: the *ah* we are using rhymes with *ma* and *pa*.

Don't worry about being too precise. This is offered as guidance only.

To make it easier, there's a video explaining all the pronunciation you need at **www.galleryofmagick.com**, on the *Pronunciation and Spelling* FAQ page.

1. Vehu

VAH-HEH-VAH

VAH is the English word *ah*, with *v* at the front. HEH starts with *h*, and then has the EH sound, which is *yeah* without the *y*.

VEH-WHO

VEH is like *yeah* with a *v* sound instead of a *y* sound. WHO is the English word *who*.

2. Yeli

YAW-LAH-YAW

YAW is like *raw*, but starting with *y* instead of *r*. LAH is the English word *ah* with an *l* at the front.

YELL-EE

YELL is the English word *yell*. EE is like *bee* without the *b*.

3. Sit

SAH-YAW-TEH

SAH is the English word *ah* with an *s* at the front. YAW is like *raw*, but starting with *y* instead of *r*. TEH is like *yeah* with a *t* sound instead of a *y* sound.

SEET

SEET is like *beet* with an *s* instead of a *b*.

4. Elem

AHLAH-MEH

AHLAH is like the English word *ah*, followed by LAH, which is simply *ah* with an *l* at the front. MEH is like *yeah* with an *m* sound instead of a *y* sound.

ELL-EM

ELL is like *bell* without the *b*. EM is like *stem* without the *st*.

5. Mahash

MEH-HEH-SHE

MEH is like *yeah* with an *m* sound instead of a *y* sound. HEH starts with *h*, and then has the EH sound, which is *yeah* without the *y*. SHE is the English word *she*.

MAH-HAHSH

MAH is the English word *ah* with an *m* at the front. HAHSH sound like *harsh* but with a much softer *r*. Put an *h* in front of the English word *ah*, with a *sh* sound on the end.

6. Lelah

LAH-LAH-HEH

LAH is the English word *ah* with an *l* at the front. HEH starts with *h*, and then has the EH sound, which is *yeah* without the *y*.

LEH-LAH

To get LEH, take the word *yeah*, and put an *l* sound in place of the *y* sound. LAH is the English word *ah* with an *l* at the front.

7. Acha

ACK-AH-AH

ACK is like *back* without the *b*. AH is like the English word *ah*.

ACH-AH

ACH uses the CH sound described above, and sounds like the *ach* in *Rachmaninoff*. AH is like the English word *ah*.

8. Kahet

KAH-HEH-TAH

For KAH use the English word *ah* with a *k* at the front. HEH starts with *h*, and then has the EH sound, which is *yeah* without the *y*. TAH is the English word *ah* with a *t* at the front.

KAH-HET

For KAH use the English word *ah* with a *k* at the front. HET is like *bet* with an *h* instead of a **b**.

9. Hezi

HEH-ZAH-YAW

HEH starts with *h*, and then has the EH sound, which is *yeah* without the *y*. ZAH is like the English word *ah*, with a *z* at the front. YAW is like *raw*, but starting with *y* instead of *r*.

HEH-ZEE
HEH starts with *h*, and then has the EH sound, which is *yeah* without the *y*. ZEE is like *see* with a *z* instead of an *s*.

10. Elad

AHLAH-DAH
AHLAH is like the English word *ah*, followed by LAH, which is simply *ah* with an *l* at the front. For DAH, put a *d* in front of the English word *ah*.

ELL-AHD
ELL is like *bell* without the *b*. AHD is like the English word *ah* with a *d* on the end.

11. Lav

LAH-AHVAH
LAH is the English word *ah* with an *l* at the front. AHVAH is like the English word *ah*, followed by a *v* sound, and then *ah* again.

LAHV
LAVH is the English word *ah*, with an *l* at the front and a *v* at the end. It rhymes with *carve*.

12. Haha

HEH-HEH-AH
HEH starts with *h*, and then has the EH sound, which is *yeah* without the *y*. AH is like the English word *ah*.

HAH-AH
For HAH, put an *h* at the front of the English word *ah*. AH is like the English word *ah*.

13. Yezel

YAW-ZAH-LAH
YAW is like *raw*, but starting with *y* instead of *r*. ZAH is like the English word *ah*, with a *z* at the front. LAH is the English word *ah* with an *l* at the front.

YEH-ZELL
YEH is like *yeah*. ZELL is like *bell*, with a *z* instead of a *b*.

14. Mebah

MEH-BEH-HEH

MEH is like *yeah* with an *m* sound instead of a *y* sound. BEH is like *bet* without the *t*. HEH starts with *h*, and then has the EH sound, which is *yeah* without the *y*.

MEB-AH

MEB is like the English word *ebb*, with an *m* at the front. AH is like the English word *ah*.

15. Hari

HEH-REH-YAW

HEH starts with *h*, and then has the EH sound, which is *yeah* without the *y*. REH is like *yeah* with an *r* sound instead of a *y* sound. YAW is like *raw*, but starting with *y* instead of *r*.

HAH-REE

For HAH, put an *h* at the front of the English word *ah*. REE is like *bee*, but with an *r* instead of a *b*.

16. Hakem

HEH-KAW-MEH

HEH starts with *h*, and then has the EH sound, which is *yeah* without the *y*. KAW sounds like the *caw* of a crow. Take the word *awe* and put a *k* sound at the front. MEH is like *yeah* with an *m* sound instead of a *y* sound.

HAH-KEM

For HAH, put an *h* at the front of the English word *ah*. KEM is *gem* with a *k* instead of a *g*.

17. Lav

LAH-AHVAH

LAH is the English word *ah* with an *l* at the front. AHVAH is like the English word *ah*, followed by a *v* sound, and then *ah* again.

LAHV

LAVH is the English word *ah*, with an *l* at the front and a *v* at the end. It rhymes with *carve*.

18. Keli

KAH-LAH-YAW

For KAH use the English word *ah* with a *k* at the front. LAH is the English word *ah* with an *l* at the front. YAW is like *raw*, but starting with *y* instead of *r*.

KEH-LEE

To get KEH, take the word *yeah* and put a *k* sound in place of the *y* sound. LEE sounds exactly as written, and rhymes with *tree*.

19. Lov

LAH-VAH-VAH

LAH is the English word *ah* with an *l* at the front. VAH is the English word *ah*, with *v* at the front.

LAWV

LAWV is the English word *law* with a *v* at the end.

20. Pahal

PEH-HEH-LAH

PEH is like *yeah* with a *p* sound instead of a *y* sound. HEH starts with *h*, and then has the EH sound, which is *yeah* without the *y*. LAH is the English word *ah* with an *l* at the front.

PAH-HAHL

PAH is the English word *ah* with a *p* at the front. HAHL rhymes with *Carl*, and you make it by adding an *h* to the front of the English word *ah*, and adding an *l* at the end.

21. Nelach

NOO-LAH-KAH

NOO is like *too* with an *n* instead of a *t*. LAH is the English word *ah* with an *l* at the front. For KAH use the English word *ah* with a *k* at the front.

NEH-LACH

NEH is like *yeah* with an *n* sound instead of a *y* sound. LACH is like *lap*, but replacing the *p* with the CH sound.

22. Yeyay

YAW-YAW-YAW
YAW is like *raw*, but starting with *y* instead of *r*.

YEH-YAY
YEH is like *yeah*. YAY is like *day*, but starting with *y* instead of *d*.

23. Melah

MEH-LAH-HEH
MEH is like *yeah* with an *m* sound instead of a *y* sound. LAH is the English word *ah* with an *l* at the front. HEH starts with *h*, and then has the EH sound, which is *yeah* without the *y*.

MEH-LAH
MEH is like *yeah* with an *m* sound instead of a *y* sound. LAH is the English word *ah* with an *l* at the front.

24. Chaho

CHEH-HEH-VAH
CHEH uses the CH sound described above, followed by EH (which is like *yeah* without the *y*.) HEH starts with *h*, and then has the EH sound, which is *yeah* without the *y*. VAH is the English word *ah*, with *v* at the front.

CHAH-HAW
CHAH starts with the CH sound, and ends with the word *ah*. HAW is like *paw* with an *h* instead of a *p*.

25. Netah

NOO-TAH-HEH
NOO is like *too* with an *n* instead of a *t*. TAH is the English word *ah* with a *t* at the front. HEH starts with *h*, and then has the EH sound, which is *yeah* without the *y*.

NET-AH
NET is the English word *net*. AH is like the English word *ah*.

26. Haah

HEH-AH-AH
HEH starts with *h*, and then has the EH sound, which is *yeah* without the *y*. AH is like the English word *ah*.

HAH-AH
For HAH, put an *h* at the front of the English word *ah*. AH is like the English word *ah*.

27. Yeret

YAW-REH-TAH
YAW is like *raw*, but starting with *y* instead of *r*. REH is like *yeah* with an *r* sound instead of a *y* sound. TAH is the English word *ah* with a *t* at the front.

YEH-RET
YEH is like *yeah*. RET is like *bet* with an *r* instead of a *b*.

28. Shaah

SHE-AH-EH
SHE is the English word *she*. AH is like the English word *ah*. EH is like the English word *eh* (the slang for *pardon*). If you are not familiar with that sound, it is the same as the *e* in *set*. Or you can think of it as *yeah* without the *y*.

SHAH-AH
SHAH is the English word *ah*, with the *sh* sound at the front. AH is like the English word *ah*.

29. Riyi

REH-YAW-YAW
REH is like *yeah* with an *r* sound instead of a *y* sound. YAW is like *raw*, but starting with *y* instead of *r*.

REE-YEE
REE is like *bee*, but with an *r* instead of a *b*. YEE is like *see*, but with a *y* instead of an *s*.

30. Om

AHVAH-MEH

AHVAH is like the English word *ah*, followed by a *v* sound, and then *ah* again. MEH is like *yeah* with an *m* sound instead of a *y* sound.

AWM

AWM rhymes with *warm*. It sounds like *awe* with an *m* added on the end.

31. Lekav

LAH-KAH-BEH

LAH is the English word *ah* with an *l* at the front. For KAH use the English word *ah* with a *k* at the front. BEH is like *bet* without the *t*.

LEH-KAV

To get LEH, take the word *yeah,* and put an *l* sound in place of the *y* sound. For KAV, take the word *have* and put a *k* sound in place of the *h* sound.

32. Vesher

VAH-SHE-REH

VAH is the English word *ah*, with *v* at the front. SHE is the English word *she*. REH is like *yeah* with an *r* sound instead of a *y* sound.

VEH-SHAR

VEH is like *yeah* with a *v* sound instead of a *y* sound. SHAR is like *car*, but with *sh* instead of *c.*

33. Yichu

YAW-CHEH-VAH

YAW is like *raw*, but starting with *y* instead of *r*. CHEH uses the CH sound described above, followed by EH (which is like *yeah* without the *y*.) VAH is the English word *ah*, with *v* at the front.

YEE-CHOO

YEE is like *see*, but with a *y* instead of an *s*. CHOO uses the CH sound described above, followed by the OO in *fool*.

34. Lahach

LAH-HEH-CHEH

LAH is the English word *ah* with an *l* at the front.

HEH starts with *h*, and then has the EH sound, which is *yeah* without the *y*. CHEH uses the CH sound described above, followed by EH (which is like *yeah* without the *y*.)

LUH-HACH

LUH is like the very first part of the word *lamp*, before you get to *amp*. HACH sounds similar to *hack*, but with the CH sound at the end.

35. Kevek

KAH-VAH-KAW

For KAH use the English word *ah* with a *k* at the front. VAH is the English word *ah*, with *v* at the front. KAW sounds like the *caw* of a crow. Take the word *awe* and put a *k* sound at the front.

KEH-VEK

To get KEH, take the word *yeah* and put a *k* sound in place of the *y* sound. VEK is like *peck* with a *v* instead of a *p*.

36. Menad

MEH-NOO-DAH

MEH is like *yeah* with an *m* sound instead of a *y* sound. NOO is like *too* with an *n* instead of a *t*. For DAH, put a *d* in front of the English word *ah*.

MEH-NAD

MEH is like *yeah* with an *m* sound instead of a *y* sound. NAD is the word *bad*, with an *n* instead of a *b*.

37. Ani

AH-NOO-YAW

AH is like the English word *ah*. NOO is like *too* with an **n** instead of a *t*. YAW is like *raw*, but starting with *y* instead of *r*.

AH-KNEE

AH is like the English word *ah*. KNEE is the English word *knee*.

38. Chaam

CHEH-AH-MEH

CHEH uses the CH sound described above, followed by EH (which is like *yeah* without the *y*.) AH is like the English word *ah*. MEH is like *yeah* with an *m* sound instead of a *y* sound.

CHAH-AHM

CHAH starts with the CH sound, and ends with the word *ah*. AHM is like the English word *ah* with an *m* on the end.

39. Reho

REH-HEH-AH

REH is like *yeah* with an *r* sound instead of a *y* sound. HEH starts with *h*, and then has the EH sound, which is *yeah* without the *y*. AH is like the English word *ah*.

REH-HAW

REH is like *yeah* with an *r* sound instead of a *y* sound. HAW is like *paw* with an *h* instead of a *p*.

40. Yeyiz

YAW-YAW-ZAH

YAW is like *raw*, but starting with *y* instead of *r*. ZAH is like the English word *ah*, with a *z* at the front.

YEH-YIZ

YEH is like *yeah*. YIZ is like *fizz* with a *y* instead of an *f*.

41. Hahah

HEH-HEH-HEH

HEH starts with *h*, and then has the EH sound, which is *yeah* without the *y*.

HAH-HAH-AH

For HAH, put an *h* at the front of the English word *ah*. AH is like the English word *ah*.

42. Mich

MEH-YAW-KAH

MEH is like *yeah* with an *m* sound instead of a *y* sound. YAW is like *raw*, but starting with *y* instead of *r*. For KAH use the word *ah* with *k* at the front.

MEECH

MEECH is the English word *me*, extended slightly to sound like *mee*, with the CH sound on the end.

43. Veval

VAH-VAH-LAH

VAH is the English word *ah*, with *v* at the front. LAH is the English word *ah* with an *l* at the front.

VEH-VAHL

VEH is like *yeah* with a *v* sound instead of a *y* sound. VAHL is the English word *ah*, with *v* at the front and an *l* at the end.

44. Yelah

YAW-LAH-HEH

YAW is like *raw*, but starting with *y* instead of *r*. LAH is the English word *ah* with an *l* at the front. HEH starts with *h*, and then has the EH sound, which is *yeah* without the *y*.

YEH-LAH

YEH is like *yeah*. LAH is the English word *ah* with an *l* at the front.

45. Sehahl

SEE-AHLAH

SEE is the English word *see*. AHLAH is like the English word *ah*, followed by LAH, which is simply *ah* with an *l* at the front.

SEH-AHL

SEH is like *yeah* with an *s* sound instead of a *y* sound. AHL is like the English word *ah* with an *l* on the end.

46. Ari

ARE-YAW

ARE is the word *are*. YAW is like *raw*, but starting with *y* instead of *r*.

AH-REE

AH is like the English word *ah*. REE is like *bee*, but with an *r* instead of a *b*.

47. Eshal

AH-SHE-LAH

AH is like the English word *ah*. SHE is the English word *she*. LAH is the English word *ah* with an *l* at the front.

ESH-AHL

ESH is like *mesh* without the *m*. AHL is like the English word *ah* with an *l* on the end.

48. Mih

MEH-YAW-HEH

MEH is like *yeah* with an *m* sound instead of a *y* sound. YAW is like *raw*, but starting with *y* instead of *r*. HEH starts with *h*, and then has the EH sound, which is *yeah* without the *y*.

ME-AH

ME is the English word *me*. AH is like the English word *ah*.

49. Vehu

VAH-HEH-VAH

VAH is the English word *ah*, with *v* at the front. HEH starts with *h*, and then has the EH sound, which is *yeah* without the *y*.

VEH-WHO

VEH is like *yeah* with a *v* sound instead of a *y* sound. WHO is the English word *who*.

50. Dani

DAH-NOO-YAW

For DAH, put a *d* in front of the English word *ah*. NOO is like *too* with an *n* instead of a *t*. YAW is like *raw*, but starting with *y* instead of *r*.

DAH-KNEE

For DAH, put a *d* in front of the English word *ah*. Knee is the English word *knee*.

51. Hachash

HEH-CHEH-SHE

HEH starts with *h*, and then has the EH sound, which is *yeah* without the *y*. CHEH uses the CH sound described, followed by EH. SHE is the word *she*.

HACH-AHSH

HACH sounds similar to *hack*, but with the CH sound at the end. AHSH is like the word *marsh* without an *m*. You can also think of it as the English word *ah* followed by the *sh* sound.

52. Omem

AH-MEH-MEH
AH is like the English word *ah*. MEH is like *yeah* with an *m* sound instead of a *y* sound.

AWM-EM
AWM rhymes with *warm*. It sounds like *awe* with an *m* added on the end. EM is like *stem* without the *st*.

53. Nena

NOO-NOO-AH
NOO is like *too* with an **n** instead of a *t*. AH is like the English word *ah*.

NEH-NAH
NEH is like *yeah* with an *n* sound instead of a *y* sound. NAH rhymes with **bar**, but is extended slightly to sound like the *Ahhhh* you say when you see a beautiful baby, but with an *n* at the beginning.

54. Nit

NOO-YAW-TAH
NOO is like *too* with an **n** instead of a *t*. YAW is like *raw*, but starting with *y* instead of *r*. TAH is the English word *ah* with a *t* at the front.

NEET
NEET is like *beet* with an *n* instead of a *b*.

55. Mivah

MEH-BEH-HEH
MEH is like *yeah* with an *m* sound instead of a *y* sound. BEH is like *bet* without the *t*. HEH starts with *h,* and then has the EH sound, which is *yeah* without the *y*.

ME-VAH
ME is the English word *me*. VAH is the English word *ah*, with *v* at the front.

56. Poi

PEH-VAH-YAW
PEH is like *yeah* with a *p* sound instead of a *y* sound.

VAH is the English word *ah*, with *v* at the front.

YAW is like *raw*, but starting with *y* instead of *r*.

PAW-EE

PAW is the English word *paw*. EE is like *bee* without the *b*.

57. Nemem

NOO-MEH-MEH

NOO is like *too* with an **n** instead of a *t*. MEH is like *yeah* with an *m* sound instead of a *y* sound.

NEM-EM

NEM is like *gem* with an *n* instead of a *g*. EM is like *stem* without the *st*.

58. Yeyil

YAW-LAH-LAH

YAW is like *raw*, but starting with *y* instead of *r*. LAH is the English word *ah* with an *l* at the front.

YEH-YEEL

YEH is like *yeah*. YEEL is like *peel* with a *y* instead of a *p*.

59. Harach

HEH-REH-CHEH

HEH starts with *h*, and then has the EH sound, which is *yeah* without the *y*. REH is like *yeah* with an *r* sound instead of a *y* sound. CHEH uses the CH sound described above, followed by EH (which is like *yeah* without the *y*.)

HAH-RAHCH

For HAH, put an *h* at the front of the English word *ah*. RAHCH is the English word *ah*, with an *r* at the front, and then ending with the CH sound.

60. Metzer

MEH-TZAH-REH

MEH is like *yeah* with an *m* sound instead of a *y* sound. TZ is like the final part of *rats*. The English word *ah* is added at the end. REH is like *yeah* with an *r* sound instead of a *y* sound.

METZUR

To get METZ you take the word *met,* and add the *ts* from *cats* to the end. You then add *ur,* which sounds like *purr* without the *p.*

61. Umab

VAH-MEH-BEH

VAH is the English word *ah,* with *v* at the front. MEH is like *yeah* with an *m* sound instead of a *y* sound. BEH is like *bet* without the *t.*

OOM-AHB

OOM is like *room* without the *r.* AHB is like the English word *ah* with a *b* on the end.

62. Yahah

YAW-HEH-HEH

YAW is like *raw,* but starting with *y* instead of *r.* HEH starts with *h,* and then has the EH sound, which is *yeah* without the *y.*

YAH-HAH

YAH is the English word *ah,* with a *y* at the front. For HAH, put an *h* at the front of the English word *ah.*

63. Anu

AH-NOO-VAH

AH is like the English word *ah.* NOO is like *too* with an *n* instead of a *t.* VAH is the English word *ah,* with *v* at the front.

AH-NOO

AH is like the English word *ah.* NOO is like *too* with an *n* instead of a *t.*

64. Machi

MEH-CHEH-YAW

MEH is like *yeah* with an *m* sound instead of a *y* sound. CHEH uses the CH sound described above, followed by EH (which is like *yeah* without the *y.*) YAW is like *raw,* but starting with *y* instead of *r.*

MAH-CHEE

MAH is the English word *ah* with an *m* at the front. CHEE uses the CH sound described above, followed by EE.

65. Dameb

DAH-MEH-BEH

For DAH, put a *d* in front of the English word *ah*. MEH is like *yeah* with an *m* sound instead of a *y* sound. BEH is like *bet* without the *t*.

DAH-MEB

For DAH, put a *d* in front of the English word *ah*. MEB is like the English word *ebb*, with an *m* at the front.

66. Menak

MEH-NOO-KAW

MEH is like *yeah* with an *m* sound instead of a *y* sound. NOO is like *too* with an *n* instead of a *t*. KAW sounds like the *caw* of a crow. Take the word *awe* and put a *k* sound at the front.

MEH-NAHK

MEH is like *yeah* with an *m* sound instead of a *y* sound. Take the English word *ah* and add an *n* at the front and a *k* at the end.

67. Iyah

AH-YAW-AH

AH is like the English word *ah*. YAW is like *raw*, but starting with *y* instead of *r*.

EE-AH

EE is like *bee* without the *b*. YAW is like *raw*, but starting with *y* instead of *r*.

68. Chavu

CHEH-BEH-VAH

CHEH uses the CH sound described above, followed by EH (which is like *yeah* without the *y*.) BEH is like *bet* without the *t*. VAH is the English word *ah*, with *v* at the front.

CHAH-VOO

CHAH starts with the CH sound, and ends with the word *ah*. VOO is like *zoo*, with a *v* instead of a *z*.

69. Raah

REH-AH-HEH
REH is like *yeah* with an *r* sound instead of a *y* sound. AH is like the English word *ah*. HEH starts with *h*, and then has the EH sound, which is *yeah* without the *y*.

RAH-AH
RAH is the word *ah* with an *r* at the front. AH is like the English word *ah*.

70. Yabam

YAW-BEH-MEH
YAW is like *raw*, but starting with *y* instead of *r*. BEH is like *bet* without the *t*. MEH is like *yeah* with an *m* sound instead of a *y* sound.

YAH-BAHM
YAH is the English word *ah*, with a *y* at the front. For BAHM, put a *b* in front of the English word *ah* and add an *m* at the end.

71. Hayi

HEH-YAW-YAW
HEH starts with *h*, and then has the EH sound, which is *yeah* without the *y*. YAW is like *raw*, but starting with *y* instead of *r*.

HAH-YEE
For HAH, put an *h* at the front of the English word *ah*. YEE is like *see*, but with a *y* instead of an *s*.

72. Mum

MEH-VAH-MEH
MEH is like *yeah* with an *m* sound instead of a *y* sound. VAH is the English word *ah*, with *v* at the front.

MOOM
MOOM like *moon* ending with an *m* instead of an *n*.

When Magick Works

If you have questions, our website is an excellent source of background material and practical posts that help you to get magick working. We could have published two or three books on magickal practice, but instead, it's all there for free. You can also find extensive FAQs for every book. I urge you to make good use of the site when you encounter problems, and also when you wish to expand your understanding of magick.

There are new posts every few weeks, and they can help keep your magick vital and hone your understanding.

The Gallery of Magick Facebook page will also keep you up to date. Please note that we only have one official Facebook page, and information in various fan groups is not always accurate.

If you have an interest in developing your magick further, there are many texts that can assist you, covering everything from money magic to archangels. Please visit our website to find out more.

www.galleryofmagick.com

I'm also a composer, and I've created orchestral angel music, based on my direct contact with angels. The music can help you to sense the presence of an angel, or can be used to find the right mood for your magic. You can hear the music at my website.

www.zannablaise.com

Love, *Zanna*

30696751R00116

Printed in Poland
by Amazon Fulfillment
Poland Sp. z o.o., Wrocław